W9-BBD-854

PRINT CASEBOOKS 2/SECOND ANNUAL EDITION
THE BEST IN COVERS & POSTERS

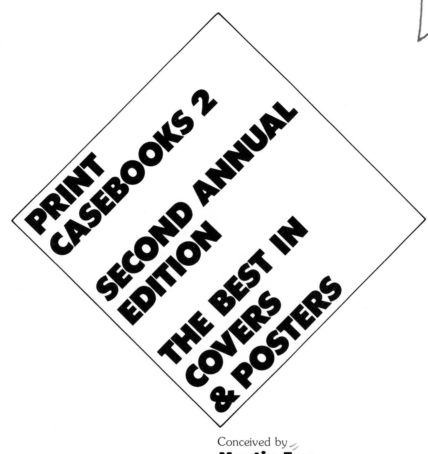

PRINT CASEBOOKS 2 SECOND ANNUAL EDITION THE BEST IN COVERS & POSTERS

Conceived by
Martin Fox

Text and Introduction by
Carol Stevens Kner
with
Valerie F. Brooks

Published by
**RC Publications, Inc.
Washington, D.C.**

Published by RC Publications, Inc. 6400 Goldsboro Road NW Washington, D.C. 20034

Manufactured in U.S.A. First Printing 1977

PRINT CASEBOOKS 2/SECOND ANNUAL EDITION/THE BEST IN COVERS & POSTERS
Library of Congress Catalog Card Number 76-395-85
ISBN 0-915734-16-8

PRINT CASEBOOKS 2/SECOND ANNUAL EDITION
Complete 6-Volume Set
ISBN 0-915734-10-9

RC PUBLICATIONS
President and Publisher: Robert Cadel
Vice President and Editor: Martin Fox
Art Director/Designer: Andrew P. Kner
Assistant Editor: Ellen-Jane Opat
Associate Art Director: Carol Stevens Kner
Business Manager: Howard Cadel
Title Page Illustration: Isadore Seltzer

When the first edition of the Print Casebooks was published in 1975, posters were discussed in one volume and covers in another. This year, although posters and covers were judged as two separate categories, they were all reviewed on the same day by the same jury and the results of that session have been put together in a single book. The combination is entirely logical. Although there are some obvious differences between the two categories, a cover is, after all, essentially a small poster, designed to attract attention and convey information quickly, clearly, and as handsomely as possible.

The decision to take advantage of the natural alliance of these two categories, and publish the results of the cover and poster competitions together, posed a problem for editors and jury alike. A great deal of good material was submitted, and even before the judging took place it was apparent that making the final choices was going to be difficult. To accommodate what they expected to be an unusually large number of chosen entries, the editors decided to make the Best in Covers & Posters somewhat longer than standard Casebook length. The judges worked hard to be as selective as possible to fit the space available. The final result of their deliberations is a collection of outstanding work, a truly representative selection of the best covers and posters produced in the U.S. and Canada during the past 18 months.

The 90-odd selections discussed here are interesting on one level as a kind of sociological documentation of contemporary life, reflecting the enormous variety of cultural interests, publications, educational opportunities, popular entertainments, and commercial ventures which preoccupy our society. On a more specific level, from the point of view of design, they represent a wide range of graphic media, artistic techniques and individual expression. Like the judges of the first Casebook competition, this year's jury seemed to be disturbed by the eclecticism. After the dazzling innovations of the '60s when, with the economic boom as a catalyst, several specific trends took the country by storm, the design of the '70s seemed to some of them both undefinable and too safe. "There doesn't seem to be any specific direction," commented Seymour Chwast, "no style of the '70s. Book jackets are down; advertising is waiting for something to happen. Posters run the gamut from crude to slick, like a survey of every kind of poster." And Mike Gross remarked, "Nothing is inspired; I think it's a reflection of the economy. There are very few specific directions."

Aside from this general lament, and perhaps because there is no definite contemporary style, the judges opinions about just what is happening were somewhat contradictory. Chwast asserted that "record covers have been good for some time; that's the most interesting area of design. Unlike magazine covers where everything has to fit into a mold, record album designs don't have to express the personality of the label." Gross agreed that "record albums are consistently so good and so varied that it's hard to find one better than the others." But Paul Bacon felt otherwise. "Album covers are not beautifully done when you examine them closely," he said. "They have a 'quicky' quality. Trying hard to be outrageous becomes boring." Both Bacon and Gross were impressed by the number of good posters submitted, Bacon asserting that "posters were the stars of the competition." Bill Cadge, on the other hand, complained that "basically very few really good posters are being done, though there are some."

This very lack of consensus, together with the variety and eclecticism of the material the judges discussed, reveals something about the nature of design in the mid-'70s. In a society where it is possible for a woman to be equally fashionable in a pants suit, a long skirt, or knickers and boots, it is hardly surprising that the prevailing state of graphic design allows for everything from nostalgically realistic illustration to Art Deco stylization to classical typography to funky, three-dimensional sculpture. Quite simply, anything goes. The wild experimentation of the '60s may be over; perhaps economic pressures have reduced the number of risks designers are willing or able to take (though some of the innovative designs published here were produced on a shoestring), but the range of styles and techniques, the variety of possible solutions to similar problems is greater than ever before.

Such diversity is this Casebook's *raison d'être*. In the early '60s, it wasn't necessary to ask why a designer chose to set copy in Helvetica and base his layout on a geometric grid. Swiss graphics were in. Likewise, a certain amount of psychedelically inspired illustration was *de rigeur* in the late '60s. Expanding options, however, and the lack of any one style that can accurately be called fashionable today make it all the more interesting to find out just how the designers and art directors whose work is featured in this book arrived at these particular solutions.

Some of them were understandably reluctant to discuss that private process in which ideas are considered and rejected almost instinctively, without conscious method, until the final answer presents itself. For them, perhaps, as in the German expression *"es geht mir Licht auf,"* the design is born full-fledged and there is no process to discuss. Or, it may be that having produced the work, they feel it should speak for itself without explanation. The more communicative designers, however, have given us a

valuable insight into the creative process, and in so doing have not only helped us to interpret their own work, but have also enriched our understanding of design as a profession.

It may be unfair to draw wholesale general conclusions from the questionnaires returned with the selected entries, since detailed information about the entries that were not chosen is unavailable. It is true, however, that most of the responses suggested that the designer was given considerable if not unlimited freedom in working out the problem. When copywriters and clients were involved in the solution, it was always in a supportive or collaborative capacity rather than a judicial or critical one. Perhaps the lack of a '70s style noted by the judges is one result of that liberty. This writer finds such individuality more to be applauded than deplored. Could there be a more appropriate common denominator for work produced during the Bicentennial celebration of a nation founded on the concept of individual freedom?

—*Carol Stevens Kner*

Seymour Chwast

Chwast was a founding partner of Push Pin Studios and of the studio's publication, Push Pin Graphic. His illustrations, posters and animated drawings have received a variety of applications, including print and television advertising, packaging design, book and record album jackets and magazines; several of his posters are in the Museum of Modern Art collection. In 1970, Chwast's and Push Pin's work was exhibited at a two-month-long retrospective exhibition at the Louvre's Musée des Art Décoratifs.

Bill Cadge

Following a 26-year career as an art director, Bill Cadge is currently a free-lance photographer in New York City. Before that, he was art director at Redbook, where he completely redesigned the magazine's logo and format. He has been associate art director at McCall's, art director in the sales promotion department at Doyle Dane Bernbach, and assistant art director for Women's Home Companion and the Philadelphia Evening Bulletin promotion department.

Paul Bacon

Bacon has been designing book jackets since forming his own studio in the mid-1950s. Before that, he designed record album covers, wrote for jazz magazines and studied at S.W. Hayter's Atelier 17. His introduction to the design field was in Hal Zamboni's studio where he apprenticed for several years.

Michael Gross

Gross, a principal with the design firm of Pellegrini, Kaestle & Gross, has spent most of his professional life designing for magazines. He worked for Cosmopolitan, Medical Economics, Hospital Physician, Eye and Family Health magazines, and for five years he art-directed National Lampoon. His firm now designs covers for Esquire, books, record jackets, magazine formats, annual reports, and produces live and animated films.

An intricate network of loops and swirls, gracefully attached to the lower half of an unmistakably Victorian face, serves as both title and illustration for this ''fascinating history of beards through the ages.'' In one of those all too rare one-sketch/no-controversy transactions that proves the ''rightness'' of the design, art director Harris Lewine and designer Alan Peckolick managed to create a book cover which suggests an infinite variety of facial hair styles while avoiding the depiction of any single one of them. Simple and direct, essentially a small poster designed to attract, inform and intrigue the viewer as effectively as possible, this book cover reveals a perfect collaboration between designer Peckolick and letterer Tom Carnase. It is nice to find, in this age of mechanization, that Carnase's skillfully rendered rich and curly swashes couldn't have been supplanted by any typeface.

Publisher: Harcourt Brace Jovanovich
Art director: Harris Lewine
Designer: Alan Peckolick
Letterer: Tom Carnase

Reginald Reynolds

The fascinating history of beards through the ages. "First-rate entertainment." —San Francisco Chronicle

A & M Graphics is the design division of the California-based record company of the same name. Responsible for the production of a vast number of album covers each season, A & M holds to an obvious and certainly sensible design policy that each album must be considered individually and that its design must reflect the music and personality of the artist in question, with only minimal importance, if any, given to the visual identity of the recording label itself.

   Putting this policy into practice, art director Roland Young and designer Mick Haggerty set about producing a cover for an Arthur, Hurley and Gottlieb album called *Sunlight Shinin'* with only two days allowed from concept to finished art, a time span which Young feels is fundamentally beneficial. His theory is that pressure forces the designer to think of a good solution fast, and anxiety about meeting the requirements of a limited production schedule prevents management from finding fault with the designer's solution. In this case, Young and Haggerty wanted to get across two essential ideas about this group of three young musicians—that their music is happy, light rock and that they are based in Miami. The designers decided to capitalize on the special funky character of Miami Beach architecture. Haggerty's logo is set against the cream-colored tiles of a resort hotel and to carry out the theme of "Sunlight Shinin'," the name of the first cut on the record,

Client: A & M Records
Designer: Mick Haggerty
Design firm: A & M Graphics, Hollywood, CA
Art director: Roland Young
Photographer: George Jerman

he has punctuated his illustration with shadows made by the noon sun. A casually slanted, unpretentious photograph of the performers in front of an endless strip of beachfront hotels adds to the informality of the overall design.

A & M's approach to the cover of Thad Jones and Mel Lewis' *Suite for Pops* is entirely different. A collection of original music written in memory of and as a tribute to Louis Armstrong, this album was the first in a budget jazz series, the production of which was complicated by a four-surface package which included liner notes, charts, photographs, transcriptions and illustrations. Designer Phil Shima asked David McMacken, a good, versatile illustrator not too committed to one particular style, to do a portrait of Satchmo that would somehow express the affectionate reverence of contemporary musicians for this master jazz artist. McMacken's deft use of airbrushing, indefinite detailing, and subtle highlighting of the pastel brown accomplished the required effect. Shima had to cope with an unusual number of last-minute additions and deletions in the copy, which forced him to handle the design very much like a magazine layout. Although there are now some 15 jazz albums planned for the series, Shima reports that they have no unifying design theme. "Some use illustrations, some photography, and some just type," he observes. "A unifying theme would be too

Client: A & M records
Designer: Phil Shima
Illustrator: David McMacken
Copywriter: Arnold Jay Smith (liner notes)

restrictive.''

David McMacken's considerable talents were enlisted again for the album *Tom Cat* by free-form sax player Tom Scott and the L.A. Express, released by Ode Records, a separate label distributed by A & M. Basing the cover illustration on the record's title cut, art director Chuck Beeson, having previously decided against a photographic treatment using real animals, asked McMacken to paint the group as cats whose faces were identifiable as the musicians involved. The three-week deadline made the assignment a rush job and the selection of the

illustrator was critical. There would be no time for a second chance. Beeson had worked with McMacken before and felt that he could successfully direct him in what would be a relatively demanding project. ''McMacken's style was basically a much more simplified airbrushing technique,'' Beeson explains. ''He had the draftsmanship and the eye for composition and I knew he was capable of getting into more complex overlays of art.'' McMacken's final painting of a bunch of alley-cat entertainers, making music among parked cars and garbage cans in a back lot,

involved many preliminary layers of airbrushing and the fastidious addition of detail with a one-hair brush. The success of the illustration resulted in its subsequent use as a poster.

Client: Ode Records/Lou Adler
Art director: Chuck Beeson
Illustrator: David McMacken
Letterers: Chuck Schmidt, Chuck Beeson

Over the years, Esquire's image has changed several times. Back in the '20s it was known for its fiction and humor. Subsequently, for a time, it took on the prurient aspects of a girlie magazine, featuring glossy photos of semi-dressed females, suggestive cartoons and off-color jokes. Most recently it has reasserted its intellectual status, publishing important new fiction and featuring the work of its many fine columnists. Esquire's latest scoop, a little competition for New York magazine's gossipy items about the rich, hip crowd, is the publication in serial form of Truman Capote's novel, *Answered Prayers.*

Free-lance art director Michael Gross (formerly of the National Lampoon) and designers Bob Pellegrini and David Kaestle were given the task not only to come up with a design worthy of Capote's latest installment but also to initiate a cover format change in the hope of picking up sagging newsstand sales. In their original sketch, the team pictured the diminutive but portly writer in slouch hat and black coat holding a bloody pen the size of a lance. Capote, reacting to an unkind article in New York magazine portraying him as a betrayer of confidences, wanted the image softened and made less malicious. Although they had not been required to submit a second rough, the three designers did a quick Magic Marker-on-tissue sketch of Capote cleaning his nails with a dagger. Capote loved it and Gross flew to Los Angeles to

supervise the photography.

In solving the second half of their problem, the team decided that to compete with other mass magazines whose cover illustrations zero in only on the feature story, they would begin a series of multiple-image covers in which the secondary titles were illustrated as well. Two bare heads and an egg (symbols for baldness, blacks, and cholesterol) contrast nicely with Capote's hatted, muffled figure and the whole collage is punctuated neatly at the bottom by a bare bit of leg and a fluffy pink slipper.

Although Gross feels that the cover turned out "exactly as envisioned," he found the printing below standard. The design's success on the newsstands has been proved, however. Sales were up 30 per cent over the same month in the previous year.

Publisher: Esquire Magazine
Design firm: Pellegrini, Kaestle and Gross, Inc., New York
Art director: Michael Gross
Designers: Bob Pellegrini, David Kaestle, Michael Gross
Photographer: Jim McCrary

MAY 1976
PRICE $1.50

Esquire

Capote Strikes Again!
More from
Answered Prayers:
The most talked-about book
of the year

What if your hair
had only six months
to live?

Why blacks
aren't scary
anymore

The cholesterol
war: Should
America
kill all its
chickens?

Dress like
a hooker and
charge it–page 70

Creating a cover for a graphic arts journal ought to be any designer's most welcome task. Where else can he find an audience which speaks his language, an audience so well versed in contemporary images and symbols? In what other circumstances can he operate without the restrictions of a commercial client or the hassle of committee decisions? To designer Andrew Kner, thinking up a cover for an issue of PRINT devoted to an analysis of the differences between schlock, camp, and kitsch was just such an interesting challenge. With only one month from idea to finished mechanical and absolutely no budget, he had to find a design that would comment on bad taste without sinking so low as to be in bad taste itself. "We planned this cover late in 1974," Kner recalls, "in the wake of Watergate, right after Nixon's resignation when we were all worried about the country's economic tailspin. We wanted to put together a funny image of America in trouble, one that would also relate in some way to the contents of the issue." The resulting photograph—pure, unadulterated camp—shot by Vince Aiosa for fun and credit, combines two old clichés to make one brand new image. Uncle Sam, that traditional symbol of power and prosperity, has become the bum in the railroad yard, brooding over his lonely fire, a sign of America's new depression. As Kner explains it, "By combining two clichés, we spoofed them both."

Pierre Le-Tan's cover for
PRINT, a totally different but
equally effective comment on
contemporary graphic images,
was a much easier project.
"Very often," says Kner, "we
run a major portfolio and I
ask the designer or illustrator
to do a cover, without
restrictions, except that it
should comment in some way
on the design field and art in
general." This cover,
originally done for the New
Yorker, had been rejected
without comment. Le-Tan
submitted it to Kner, who felt
that it fit PRINT's
requirements perfectly. "The
drawing is a very witty
comment on art and vanity
and the whole idea of
interpreting an image,"
explains Kner; "it is very
much a personal view but
one that all PRINT readers
can relate to."

Publisher: RC Publications, Inc.
Art director/designer: Andrew
P. Kner
January/February 1975:
Photographer: Vince Aiosa
July/August 1975:
Illustrator: Pierre Le-Tan

While we are generally accustomed to seeing violence and brutality in films, the idea of a violent, brutal act appearing on a book jacket is rather foreign. Even if that act has a symbolic as well as a literal meaning, it is still brutal, and in publishing, a relatively conservative industry, can provide an area of conflict.

Cataract is a case in point. For this memoir of life in a Soviet labor camp, art director Harris Lewine asked woodcut artist Barbara Bascove to illustrate the cover. She chose to depict the book's most frenzied and agonizing scene, a man consuming his leg while his cellmates look away hopelessly. It is, as Bascove points out, a valid allegory of the book as a whole and an overwhelming statement about all labor camps.

Lewine agreeed, but final approval had to come from the publisher, who saw and rejected a first proof. It was at this point that *Cataract*'s editor and co-publisher, Helen Wolff, who also wanted Bascove's cover, moved to save it. Largely through her efforts and Lewine's support was the cover eventually approved. After that, the only correction made by Bascove was some further delineation of the figures requested by Lewine. The three-color woodcut was completed in three weeks.

This is a powerful and uncompromising solution of a kind rarely seen, even with books and authors of even greater renown.—*VFB*

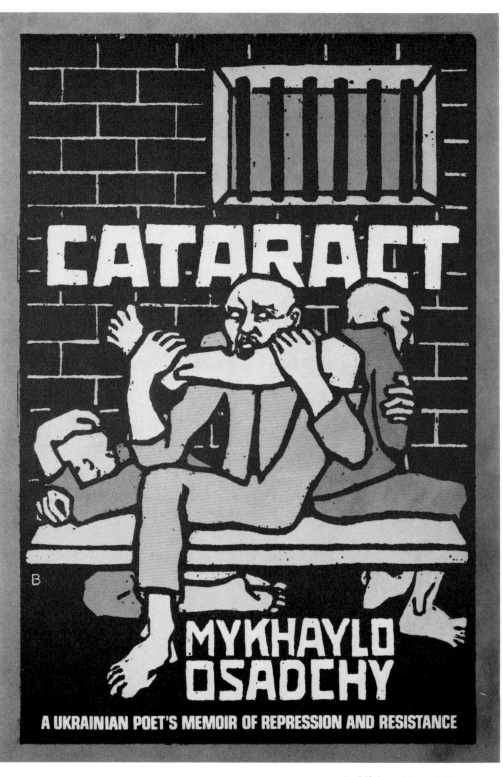

Publisher: Harcourt Brace Jovanovich
Art Director: Harris Lewine
Designer/illustrator/letterer: Barbara Bascove

Even though the Cate Bros., a blues-based country rock band, had already laid down some of the basic tracks for their first album on Asylum Records, they were still looking for several more musicians to fill out the group. Rather than illustrate the album cover with a misleading photograph of an incomplete band, the Cate Bros. manager, Ron Stone, decided to emphasize the group's logo. Besides making it easier for the public to identify the band, a strong, well-designed logo would help the group stick in the minds of radio and industry sales people and booking agents.

Designer Glen Christensen, who shared Stone's viewpoint, originally planned to do the logo as a woodcut. Basing his design on the group's down-home musical style and their Fayetteville, Arkansas, background, he decided to play up their funky aspects by decorating the lettering with a fish hook. When Christensen actually came across a rusty old fish hook, it changed the general direction of his design. After sending the hook to Gribbitt Studios for some experimental Polaroids, Christensen abandoned the woodcut idea and decided to use the hook as the "C" in the group's name, designing the rest of the letters to match. The drops of water—Gribbitt's contribution to the overall effect—were actually Karo syrup. "I had a company called ABC Letter Art in Los Angeles cut all the letters, including the large

hook, in aluminum," Christensen explains; "they were done oversize—about 20" wide overall. They also antiqued them. I went back to the studio, reset up the shot and did the finish as a 4" by 5" with a slate-colored background." Although the photographic and lettering services were additional expenses, Christensen's

budget was not severely restricted (overall budget was approximately $2000).

Now that the group's visual identity has been so successfully established, it will probably be carried over in some form on all Cate Bros. future albums.—*VFB*

Client: Asylum Records
Art director/designer: Glen Christensen
Photographer: Gribbitt Studios
Letterer: ABC Letter Art

When Verve Records decided to put out a series of period jazz recordings—new releases of its historically priceless tracks by entertainers such as Billie Holiday, Charlie Parker, Bud Powell, and Lester Young, the task of creating a format for the albums fell to Verve's art director, Beverly Parker. "It was horrible— deadly," Parker recalls; "I had one month to design and produce six record sleeves including art, copy, type and mechanicals." To make matters worse, funds for the project were as limited as the time.

Parker's solution, an ingenious kind of cheaper-by-the-dozen arrangement, resulted in covers that are not only individually effective but also maintain their special relationship as a series. Rather than commission a separate painting for each album, a process which would have been both time-consuming and expensive, Parker asked illustrator Stanislaw Zagorski to do a group portrait of the five soloists involved. She then cropped in around their heads to produce the individual front cover

THE FIRST
VERVE
SESSIONS
BILLIE
HOLIDAY

The 1952-54 recordings,
featuring Oscar Peterson,
Paul Quinichette,
Ray Brown, Charlie Shavers,
Flip Phillips, Barney Kessel
and Freddie Green.

close-ups, a concept that will be repeated as groups of future albums come up. For *Jazz at the Philharmonic,* she picked up Zagorski's wall poster, a decoration from the background of the picture of the four men, and stripped in a portion of the audience watching Billie Holiday. A small version of the entire painting appears on the back cover of each sleeve.

The extensive cover copy, an informative biographical/musical analysis of each entertainer, provided Parker not only with another challenge but also with a chance to further unify the series. To make the text as legible as possible, designer Carl Barile handled the layout like an outsize magazine spread. The copy, which begins on the back cover and continues to the inside, was separated into ruled columns, interspersed with teaser quotes and punctuated with exaggerated Bodoni initials. Repetition of the Bodoni typeface with horizontal rules and an italic blurb on the front cover unifies the pictorial and typographic elements of the overall design.

Right: Zagorski's group portrait showing five soloists and wall poster for "Jazz at the Philharmonic."

In spite of the difficulties, Parker is satisfied with the final results. ''The package in its entirety became more than an album cover,'' she observes. The design format is entirely contemporary but the softly modelled illustrations with their moody shadows and facial highlights capture the spirit of those bygone jazz decades. Even more important, the format is a durable one that will work just as well for the 100th album in the series as for the first six (four of which were selected for the Casebook).

Right: back cover of Billie Holiday album.
Far right: sample of center spread from two-record set.

Client: Polydor Records/Robert Hurwitz
Design firm: Album Graphics, Inc., New York
Art director: Beverly Parker
Designers: Carl S. Barile, Beverly Parker
Illustrator: Stanislaw Zagorski

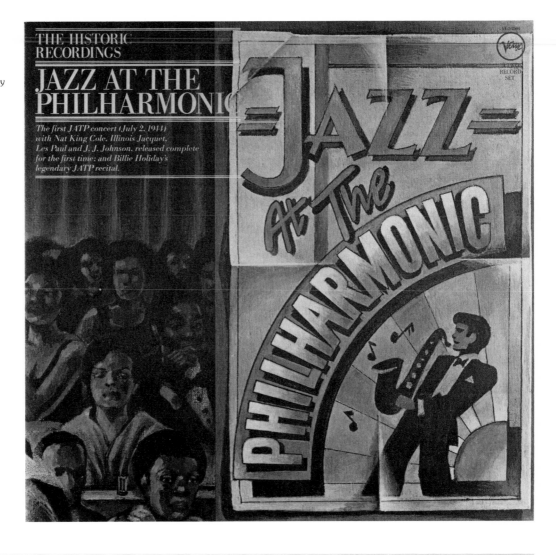

THE HISTORIC RECORDINGS

JAZZ AT THE PHILHARMONIC

The first JATP concert (July 2, 1944) with Nat King Cole, Illinois Jacquet, Les Paul and J. J. Johnson, released complete for the first time; and Billie Holiday's legendary JATP recital.

When the Mercantile Library in St. Louis, Missouri, was in need of funds recently, a decision was made to auction off its collection of George Caleb Bingham drawings, valued at nearly $2 million. The resulting public dissent was so great, though, that the governor established a fund-raising organization, Bingham Sketches, Inc., for the sole purpose of keeping the collection in Missouri. This group's primary effort, in fact, was a comprehensive exhibition of the 19-century genre painter's drawings of local river life and politicians that would travel throughout the state. The firm of Hellmuth, Obata & Kassabaum was retained to design graphics for the show as well as the usual assortment of collateral—including posters and a catalog—that goes with such projects.

Two versions of the catalog were planned. One, in soft cover, would be used as a fund-raising item, available for sale at participating museums and in bookstores. The other, a limited hardbound edition, would serve as a gift to major contributors to the campaign from the governor. Its cover printing would be on linen which was also debossed and with a Bingham drawing tipped-in.

From the start, designer Charles Reay was faced with the special budgetary problems that fund-raising efforts can impose. While there was no expenditure ceiling *per se,* Reay remained in constant awareness that

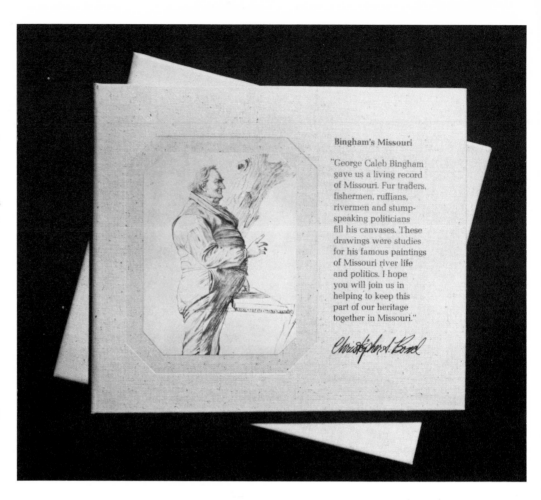

Bingham's Missouri

"George Caleb Bingham gave us a living record of Missouri. Fur traders, fishermen, ruffians, rivermen and stump-speaking politicians fill his canvases. These drawings were studies for his famous paintings of Missouri river life and politics. I hope you will join us in helping to keep this part of our heritage together in Missouri."

Christopher S. Bond

Client: Bingham Sketches, Inc.
Design firm: Hellmuth, Obata & Kassabaum, Inc., St. Louis
Designer/art director: Charles P. Reay
Copywriter: George McCue

each dollar spent at his end had to be matched in funds raised to meet the goal of $1,800,000.

In addition, while some three months were allotted for completion of all materials, Reay spent a long pre-design period with his associates on the project delving exhaustively into Bingham's life and times. Reay notes that the actual design process was "one of evolution, with the client giving approval but not making selections." Eventually, one overall approach was developed.

Although the hardbound catalog Reay produced is suitably dignified for a governor's gift, especially with its matching slipcase, he had been concerned that the type of linen selected would not accept the printing inks or debossing. Fortunately, neither problem occurred.

Reay notes that "feedback was excellent" and that he was more than pleased with the volume's appearance in that it was, as planned, compatible with the other elements in the program, and economically produced.

Incidentally, the $1,800,000 goal was met.
—VFB

Right: poster publicizing exhibition of Bingham's drawings at the St. Louis Art Museum. Below: sketch for front and back covers of catalog based on complex grid for interior layout.

Bingham's Missouri

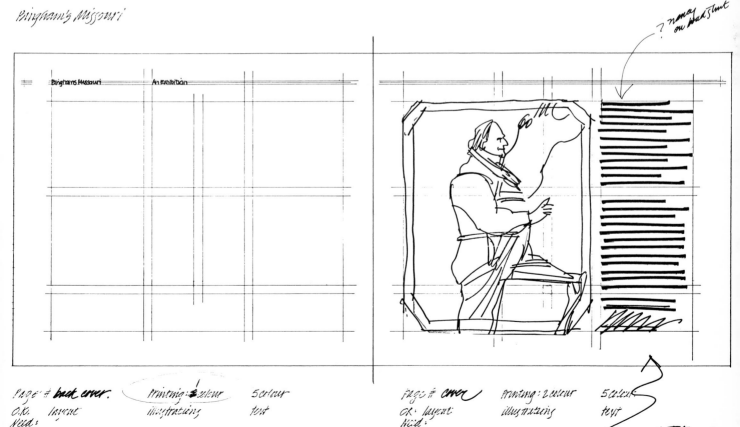

City, an attractive, newsy magazine that publisher (and noted filmmaker) Francis Ford Coppola hoped would illustrate a kind of ongoing love affair of San Franciscans with their city, was, unfortunately, a short-lived publication. Largely dependent, in a business sense, on Coppola's own personal feelings and financial backing, it was laid to rest after eight months on the newsstands, barely enough time to give it a chance. During the magazine's short life, however, prompted by a feeling that it should reflect the specific Western Victorianism that characterizes San Francisco, art director Mike Salisbury managed to produce some exceptionally good graphic design.

For the cover of an issue based on Dashiell Hammett, creator of the prototype hard-boiled private eye, Salisbury decided to glorify the image of Hammett himself rather than base his design on stylized symbols reflecting a nostalgic 1930s detective-story atmosphere. Not many good photographs of the writer existed and the one they had was fuzzy and hard to make out, so Salisbury, working with a $400 budget, asked Guy Fery to do a realistic portrait. The close-up, soft-focus romanticism of Hammett's distinguished face had great impact and Salisbury reports that this was one of City's most popular issues.

Salisbury's design for an issue devoted to WPA art projects in the San Francisco area focussed on an entirely

different aspect of the '30s. The idea was to make San Franciscans aware of an art heritage they might not know they had. Editor Warren Hinckle chose the photograph, Benny Bufano's sculpture of Florence Nightingale, and asked Salisbury to design the cover around it. Other examples of WPA art might have been used but they were murals and WPA murals exist all over the country. The work of Bufano, the best known San Francisco sculptor of the '30s, is exclusive to that area and consequently, Hinckle found it particularly appropriate. Salisbury's type layout, a negative/positive treatment designed to clarify a great deal of cover copy which had to be read across the statue, was inspired by Art Deco posters.

Publisher: City of San Francisco
Art director/designer: Mike Salisbury
Illustrator: Guy Fery ("Hammett")

When Wendell Minor was asked to design a book jacket for the novel *City of the Dead*, a story based on the New York City morgue and its chief medical examiner, he investigated research sources such as the Public Library, Culver Pictures and Wide World Photos to find appropriate visual material. Much to his surprise, nothing was available. Although he had planned to emphasize the type treatment because the publishers wanted to give the book a ''best-seller'' look, he felt that the title would be incomplete without an illustration.

With only two weeks in which to complete a comprehensive jacket sketch, Minor, with the help of art director Frank Metz, obtained permission to visit the city morgue and interview the deputy chief medical examiner, Dr. Yong Myun Rho, who had also served as medical advisor to the author. ''I took several photos of the facilities,'' Minor recalls, ''and posed cadavers to suit my layout. The finished painting was produced from this material along with color notes made on sight.'' Editor Phyllis Graham approved the final concept and the resulting picture—austere, antiseptic, gray and cold—seems, like the novel, very close to the truth.

Publisher: Simon & Schuster
Art director: Frank Metz
Designer/illustrator: Wendell Minor

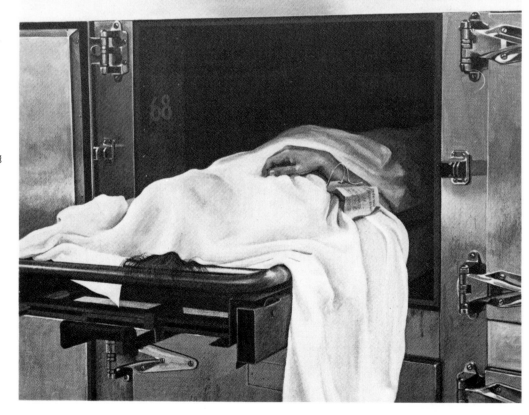

A Novel
CITY OF THE
DEAD
Herbert Lieberman

Shoulder to Shoulder

A pleasantly crowded, sepia-toned collection of old photographs, the cover of Midge Mackenzie's book, *Shoulder to Shoulder*, leaves no doubt as to the documentary nature of the volume. One of the originators of the successful BBC television series of the same title, filmmaker Mackenzie turned her copious collection of letters, journals, speeches, and pictures into a publication which would tell the story of the suffragette movement in printed form.

Because the television show and the book were essentially different statements by the same author, Knopf decided not to base the cover on the poster produced by Ivan Chermayeff for the Public Broadcasting series, but to make an entirely new design representing the special character of the book. ''The show was more a play/movie while the book was more a history,'' explains art director Bob Scudellari. ''We felt that the jacket couldn't be subtle or limited but must indicate the total scope of the book's *value*.'' Scudellari attributes the success of the cover design to the unfailing, continuous communication between author, art director and designer, who worked together on the layout of the interior pages as well. The title, printed in a bold typeface which nevertheless suggests the idiosyncrasies of turn-of-the-century, Art Nouveau lettering, provides an effective graphic image of the solidarity of the suffragettes' struggle.

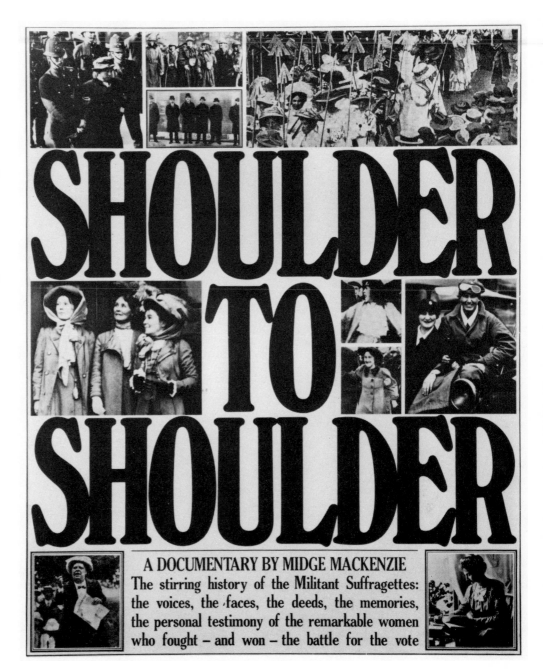

Publisher: Alfred A. Knopf
Art director: R. D. Scudellari
Designer: Louise Fili

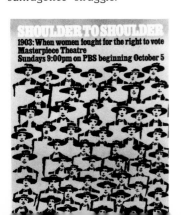

Left: poster design by Ivan Chermayeff for WNET-TV documentary series.

In September of 1975, Max Frankel, then editor of the New York Times Sunday edition, was on the lookout for an original way to illustrate a series of articles on political candidates, beginning with President Ford in November 1975 and to continue at more or less regular intervals throughout 1976. Ruth Ansel, art director of the New York Times Magazine, had recently seen the work of English sculptor Roger Law, whose caricatures of public European personalities were witty, well-designed and skillfully put together. "I wanted to publish a portfolio of Roger's work," Ansel recalls, "and Frankel suggested using him for the political series. It was really the perfect wedding of two separate ideas."

Law's first sculpture, of Ford, was made and photographed in New York. All the rest were done in London. Usually there was no manuscript, just basic outline material supplemented by phone conversations with Ansel. The only rejected sketch was a precursor to the picture of Wallace shown here with his paralyzed legs flamboyantly shrouded in a Confederate flag. To illustrate an article depicting the Alabama governor as a spicy performer who enjoys giving the press something juicy to report about, Law made Wallace into a vaudevillian song-and-dance-man in a standing position on a stage. "Too many editors took it too literally," Ansel recalls, "and thought it offensive in light of Wallace's condition.

Otherwise the project was very easy," she observes. "Roger really needs no supervision; all he needs is the right idea. Since the sketches were followed quite faithfully, there were no surprises."

Law, with his assistant, Peter Fluck, makes the figures out of soft clay, which cannot be preserved. The heads are more or less life-size, painted, and gussied up with medical eyes, teeth, wigs, and intricately stitched cloth costumes. The finished art is a color photograph.

Opposite page: winning cover selected by Casebook judges. Above: sketch for Reagan cover. Top right and right: two other covers in series.

Publisher: The New York Times Magazine
Art director/designer: Ruth Ansel
Illustrators: Roger Law, Peter Fluck

It is unusual for a trade magazine, particularly one which reports about the affairs of an industry not associated in any way with the visual arts, to maintain such high standards of graphic design. That Industrial Launderer does is a tribute to art director Jack Lefkowitz and the editors with whom he works. "IL is a management magazine for people who run uniform rental and other cleaning rental services," explains Lefkowitz. "We feel that these people need to be highly stimulated by something provocative or they won't bother opening up the book. We try to do what they won't expect and we've found from past experience that if the covers confuse them, they'll read the magazine to see what it's all about."

Lefkowitz and his wife work as a team on the cover designs. To make the most of four-color printing without incurring the cost of camera separations, Pam Lefkowitz hand-separates the finished art. Their solutions feature colorful contemporary graphic techniques and symbols but stop short of avant garde or abstract solutions that might dampen the enthusiasm of the readership. To illustrate a feature story about emblem adhesives for the March 1975 issue, Lefkowitz produced the multiple image of a shirt covered with decorative insignia. "To test emblem adhesives, several shirts are covered with test emblems and laundered repeatedly," says Lefkowitz. This was certainly an image IL readers

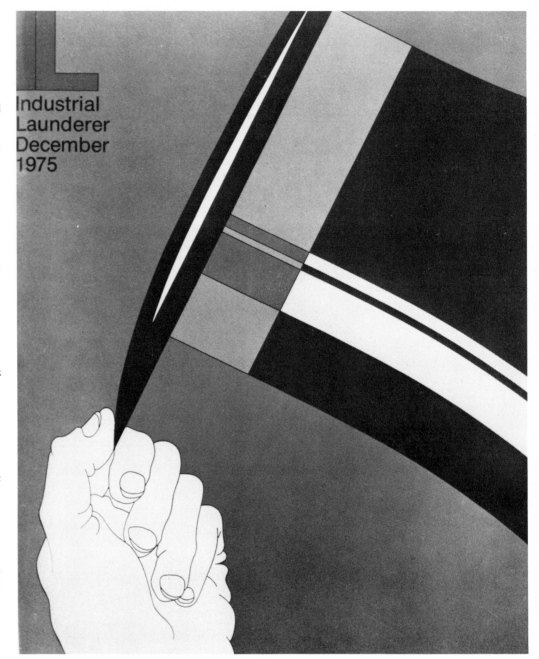

Industrial
Launderer
December
1975

Industrial
Launderer
Summer
1975

could understand.

A more whimsical design, for the summer issue of 1975, deals nevertheless with the hard facts of the industry's structure. The baby mushrooms represent small associations growing up under the protection of the National Association. The butterfly, the ocher sun and the warm orange background help convey the mood of a season when everything moves just a little bit more slowly.

To understand the concept behind the cover of the December 1975 issue, it is necessary to know something about the makeup of the Institute of Industrial Launderers. It is a kind of hierarchical parent organization in which unpaid members serve for a year or two on committees which investigate various areas of general importance to the industry such as research, technical developments, administrative procedures and new methods of marketing. The top of the hierarchy is made up of a volunteer president and board of directors. The cover illustrates an article reviewing the industry's year-end convention where all the volunteer chairmen and board members were honored for their services. "A tip of the hat," says Lefkowitz, "seemed appropriate."

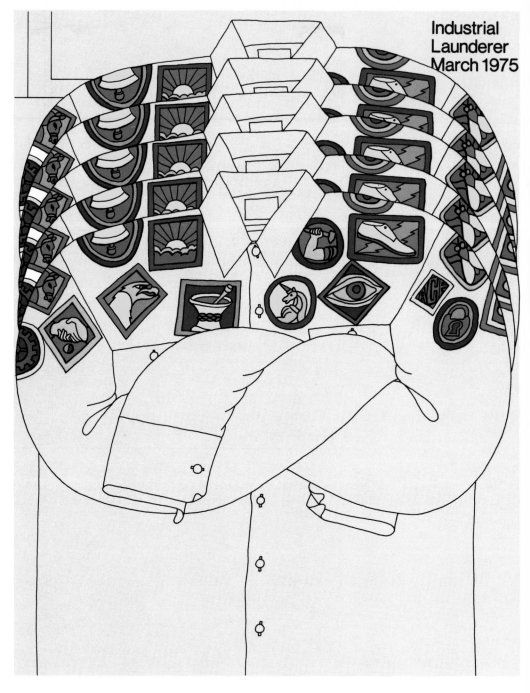

Industrial
Launderer
March 1975

Publisher: Industrial Launderer
Art director/designer: Jack Lefkowitz
Illustrator: Pam Lefkowitz

Images and Intentions

A tawny lion stands alone in the cool green foliage at the edge of a riverbank. His reflection, however, is not that of the powerful king of the beasts, but instead, the image of a mild white lamb. Glowing with imaginative grace and whimsical realism, this painting would have been a lovely illustration for a collection of fairy tales. Instead, it makes a remarkably original cover for a book entitled *Images and Intentions*, a catalog of the work of Canadian design firm Burns and Cooper. A house promotional booklet to show prospective clients and people in the design industry who Burns and Cooper are and what sort of work they do, *Images and Intentions* presents the firm's solutions to a broad spectrum of design problems, including packaging, letterhead design, direct mail advertising campaigns and corporate identity programs.

In determining an appropriate image for their own promotion piece, Cooper and Burns decided to focus on just that problem, the question of corporate identity. Heather Cooper's tawny lion represents the company, which thinks of itself as forceful and dynamic, whereas its image is in reality quite the opposite. Though not a fairy tale, the story does have a happy ending. *Images and Intentions* has been so successful that numerous requests for it have come from all sorts of businesses and institutions. Furthermore, the book is retailing for $7.95 a copy in Toronto bookstores.

Images & Intentions

The Work of Burns & Cooper Limited

Client: Burns and Cooper Ltd.
Art director/designer: Robert Burns
Designer: Jim Donoahue
Illustrator: Heather Cooper

The Afro-Eurasian Eclipse

Fantasy F9498

During the last ten years of his life, Duke Ellington travelled extensively all over the world studying the various peoples of Africa, Asia and Europe, and recording his observations, when he got back home, in musical form. *The Afro-Eurasian Eclipse*, a suite in eight parts for jazz orchestra, was the final version of Ellington's musical record of his travels. In it, he has turned his impressions into an instrumental statement that includes his own translation of out-of-the-way musical experiences, such as Australian aboriginal rhythms and African drum solos, into forms which are suitable for the American performers who interpret his music.

When Fantasy Records bought the rights to this music from Ellington's estate, the management decided to keep the budget for the album low. Although Ellington was a monumental performer, Fantasy didn't expect a great deal in the way of income from the album and the budget for each release is directly proportionate to the expected return. It was decided that the design should be an in-house project and that the art would be limited to the use of illustrative material already in existence.

At about the same time the Ellington project was getting underway, art director Phil Carroll happened to borrow a book of old German engravings from the University of California library. A catalog of ethnic types observed and documented during the travels

of some 19th-century artist/historian, the book offered page after page of profiles and frontal views representing people from many different varieties of African tribes, nomadic Arabic communities and oriental civilizations. When the Ellington album was finally assigned a title, Carroll realized that some of these fantastic illustrations would make a perfect cover. The design was put together with photostats, and the separations were made directly from the book. The

resulting panorama of meticulously detailed facial characteristics and tribal costumes, printed in warm, natural, earthy browns and reds, makes a highly appropriate visual image for Ellington's comprehensive musical journal.

Client: Fantasy Records
Art director: Phil Carroll
Designer: Jamie Putnam

The First
Seven Days

As the title suggests, jazz pianist Jan Hammer's recording, *The First Seven Days*, is a musical interpretation of the Creation. In her preliminary sketch for the album cover, art director Paula Scher decided to illustrate the theme with Biblical and evolutionary symbols suggesting God's gathering together of the dry land and the waters, His creation of lights in the firmament, and His blessing on the living creatures to "be fruitful and multiply and fill the waters in the seas." Designer Milton Glaser, however, whose talents lie partly in never choosing the expected solution, had his own ideas. Turning to his advantage a longtime interest in Tantra and the elaborate symbology of Tantric art, he decided to illustrate the cover not with the familiar (to Western eyes) iconography of Judeo-Christian art but with images which he felt would present a much more unconventional interpretation of the Creation to Western audiences.

Tantra is a secret cult of Hinduism which first developed in Northeastern India during the 6th century. Its mystical and erotic rites and principles gave rise to the development of an intricate and specific sign language symbolizing the Tantric philosophy of man's relationship to the universe. Glaser's central image, which Scher describes as a symbol of the upward and outward struggle for life, is based on an 18th-century Indian painting representing the

creation of the universe. Other Tantric symbols include spheroids (images of the world egg, a form that is fundamental to nature and the procreation of the human race) and the serpent whose coiled shape in many Tantric paintings is symbolic of latent energy. Although these images, together with emerald green and brilliant red—colors of vital forces visible in a meditative trance—may be interpreted as Tantric, Glaser's design is not without Biblical connotations whether or not they were intended.

Viewers ignorant of Tantric symbology may identify the illustrations as suns and moons, "fowls of the air," "creeping things," and "green herbs." The black background and the ambiguous delineation

between land and water makes a highly appropriate image of an "earth without form and void...of darkness upon the face of the deep."

Scher was enthusiastic about Glaser's solution but concerned that Hammer might not accept the use of Tantric symbols. "As it turned out," Scher recalls, "it was the easiest album cover I ever sold and all by accident." Hammer also happened to be involved in the study of Tantra and immediately identified with Glaser's design.

Client: Nemperor Records/ Atlantic Recording Corp.
Art director: Paula Scher
Designer: Milton Glaser

Left: "Creation of the Universe," 18th-century Indian painting from "Tantra Art" by Ajit Mookerjee; published by Ravi Kumar.

Ride 'em Cowboy

To market a new collection of songs by contemporary rock and roll artist Paul Davis, art director Eddie Biscoe of Bang Records hit upon the idea of using a hand-embroidered denim cowboy shirt as a format for the record sleeve. The title of the album, *Ride 'em Cowboy,* appears as a label sewn under the collar and the back cover offers a facsimile representation of the shirt and its occupant's hair seen from behind. To complete the gimmick, the shirt opens up the front to reveal a sepia-tone photograph of a collection of rough-and-ready characters in a 19th-century saloon and a pair of swinging shutter doors featuring a list of each cut on the album.

Biscoe's original idea was laid out on cardboard in colored pencil. James Flournoy Holmes and David Holmes of Wonder Graphics handled the technical side of the package production including having the shirt made up and lettering the song titles in looped rope. The Bang Records staff, with Biscoe in a white Stetson and Paul Davis leaning on a rifle, posed for the photograph in an old bar in what Biscoe calls ''an underground area of Atlanta.''

Biscoe notes that the die-cutting and the embossing of the stitched welted areas on the shirt were essential to the overall concept and extremely difficult. Fortunately, however, the time element for the job (two months) was comfortable and there were no budget restrictions.

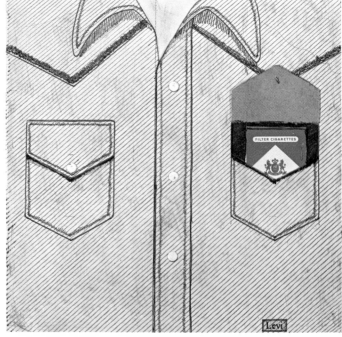

Client: Bang Records
Art director/designer: Eddie Biscoe
Packaging design: James Flournoy Holmes, David Holmes—Wonder Graphics, Inc.
Embroidery: Michele
Photographer: Nick Rietz

Top: album front. Above: album back. Right: original sketch.

To accompany an article about his work which appeared in Graphis, Richard Hess created a cover that is not only representative of his style and approach to illustration but also seems in many ways characteristically American. Against an elaborately detailed background painted in brooding tones of brown and green, a solitary blue jeans-clad figure waits at a suburban railroad station for a train that will never come. The tracks are truncated; the landscape is devoid of people; the man has only himself and his own identity to fall back on.

Part of a continuing tradition of American primitive painting which began with the 17th-century itinerant limners, worked its way through artists such as Edward Hicks and Grant Wood, and resurfaced with Grandma Moses, Hess's illustration is typical also of the naive style which has recently gained popularity among contemporary graphic designers. In this as in other examples of modern primitive illustration, the detailed landscape and flat perspective have been powerfully dramatized by the introduction of surrealist images. It is as if our traditional nostalgia for the simple life, for the long lost myths of American folklore, had been disturbed by the visitation of symbols from a bad dream.

Publisher: Graphis Press
Art director: Walter Herdeg
Illustrator: Richard Hess

Emergency Medicine, an unusually thorough monthly trade magazine (c. 260 pages per issue) financed by drug company advertising, has an unpaid circulation of 110,000 to 115,000 doctors who are involved with everyday emergency care. "The magazine is a very important educational force in medicine," asserts art director Ira Silberlicht. "It deals with life-and-death situations. Our readers really do need what we give them."

Because they have a product to sell which can result in the saving of lives, Silberlicht and his assistant, Tom Lennon, attach a great deal of importance to the design of each cover. "We read the cover story to get the gist of it," Silberlicht explains. "Every once in a while, technicalities may have to be discussed with the writer, but basically the thrust of the story determines our solution." Once the concept sketch has been approved by the executive and managing editors, Silberlicht and Lennon are free to handle the art as they please. "We want doctors to be interested enough in the cover story to read it, but," Silberlicht cautions, "too strong an image might turn them off."

The cover for the January 1975 issue, which dealt with pain, presented just such a problem. To illustrate severe suffering which overpowers to the extent that it excludes all other sensation, Silberlicht retained the services of illustrator Ed Soyka. His multiple-technique, multimedia painting depicts a

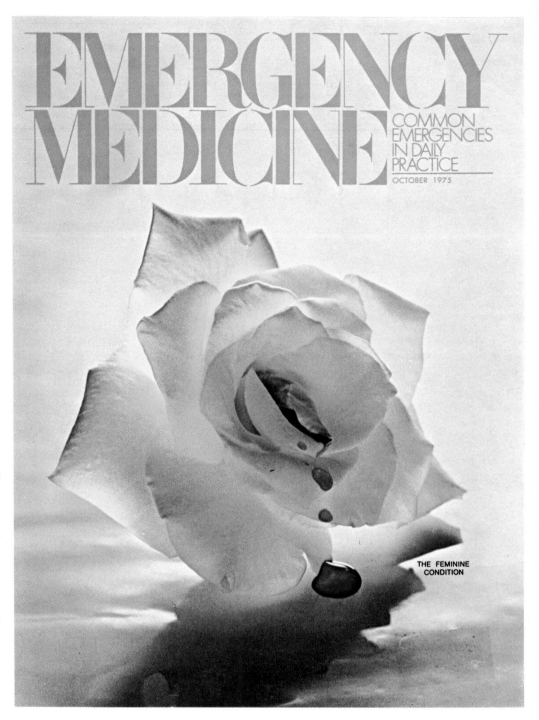

EMERGENCY MEDICINE COMMON EMERGENCIES IN DAILY PRACTICE OCTOBER 1975

THE FEMININE CONDITION

face tortured by anguish and a surrealist image of clenched teeth repeated instead of eyes. "The impact is startling," says Silberlicht, "but we probably had more difficulty getting this design approved than any other because the editors were very concerned that our readers would react negatively to it. So far, however, it has won more honors than any other piece in Emergency Medicine's history."

The problems involved in designing a cover dealing with emergency vaginal bleeding were altogether different. The topic had to be illustrated in a way which wouldn't be offensive or heavy-handed, nor could it be literal. Technical medical drawings are reproduced only inside the magazine. Silberlicht doesn't recall the first four or five ideas that preceded this solution, but he says that even the rose drew a certain amount of unfavorable comment from some of the more militant women's libbers who are among the magazine's recipients. The blood was studio blood—vegetable dyes mixed until their color and consistency satisfied the editor. "Even that presented difficulties," Silberlicht explains, "because we had to allow for the effect of the backlighting on the depth of the red."

The "Stranger in the Land" cover was in many ways the easiest of the three. An existing but unpublished piece of art—a life-size soft sculpture made largely of old nylon stockings and stuffing—the illustration had

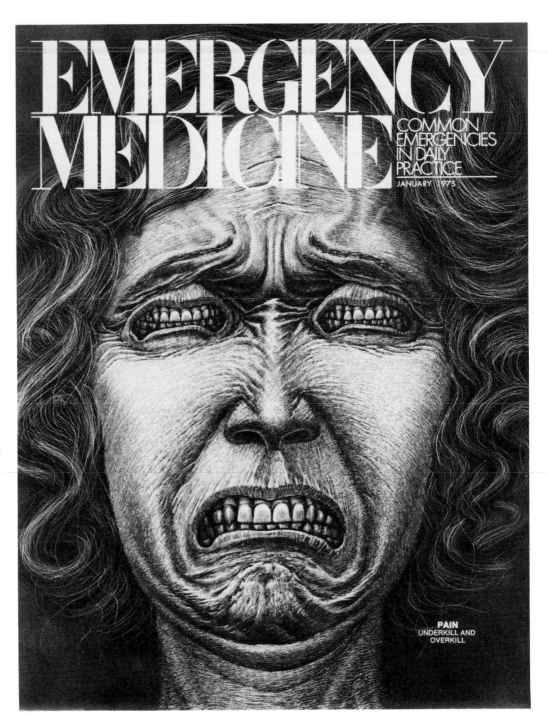

EMERGENCY MEDICINE

COMMON EMERGENCIES IN DAILY PRACTICE

JANUARY 1975

PAIN
UNDERKILL AND OVERKILL

appeared unsolicited in artist Judith Jampel's portfolio. Silberlicht filed it away hoping eventually to be able to use it. He got his chance when a cover story on old age appeared on his desk. The article cited the dramatic changes which affect the existence of older people. As their friends die, as their health fails, as their relationship to society changes, the elderly become strangers to their own former lives. The sculpture was shot in a variety of circumstances for use as interior illustration as well as on the cover. As the shooting progressed, Silberlicht and the other people involved became more and more attached to their subject. "It was an eerie experience, she was so realistic," Silberlicht observes. "She became the universal grandmother in Western culture. We all felt it. We were fortunate that photographer Eugenia Louis was available to do the shooting. Her feeling for mood and her sympathy for the plight of the aged made her an ideal choice to complete the assignment."

Publisher: Fisher Medical Publications, Inc.
Art director: Ira Silberlicht
Designer: Tom Lennon
January 1975:
Illustrator: Ed Soyka
October 1975:
Photographer: Phil Gottheil
March 1976:
Illustrator: Judith Jampel
Photographer: Eugenia Louis
Medical advisor: Eugene Y. Berger, M.D.

EMERGENCY MEDICINE
COMMON EMERGENCIES IN DAILY PRACTICE

MARCH 1976

STRANGER IN THE LAND

As a rule, authors do not have much say regarding the cover treatments of their books. *Meridian,* though, proved something of an exception.

A cover solution had been approved when the author, Alice Walker, saw a first proof and turned it down on the basis that the heroine was depicted as a Bantu African, whose features had been copied from a photograph, when her story had been about an American Southern black woman—one whom she had envisioned as more imaginatively portrayed.

Walker then requested that Barbara Bascove, the woodcut artist who had illustrated the cover for a book of Walker's poems, do a sketch for *Meridian'*s cover. Bascove found that her solution really lay in the three-part definition of the word "meridian" which the author had included in the preface to her novel, which is about ecstasy. (For example: meridian—the highest apparent point reached by a heavenly body in its course; zenith; apex; culmination.)

Bascove's approach was what she calls a "heroic profile," done as a wraparound jacket. While the woman's features are perhaps more distinctively American, the upturned face and hair yielding to wings suggest the more metaphysical or spiritual aspect that Walker also sought.

Bascove notes that her sketch was fully accepted. In addition, having received complete freedom from the art director for her cover treatment, she was able to use four-color instead of three-color as originally planned. As Bascove explains, her purpose in doing this was to create the "vibrancy of the feeling of flying." As a result, both Walker and art director Harris Lewine agreed that her cover provided the proper complement to the emotional content of the novel.—*VFB*

Publisher: Harcourt Brace Jovanovich
Art director: Harris Lewine
Designer/illustrator/letterer: Barbara Bascove

New York magazine's art director, Walter Bernard, says that covers of his magazine are "no big deal"; they're often last-on-the-list jobs that the illustrator or photographer has to complete in three or four days from receipt of the sketch. Bernard doesn't see the cover as a highlight—and he's right, it's not. But occasionally covers come along, especially some of the illustrated ones, that stand out strikingly on the newsstand.

For instance, Richard Hess's painting for "Calling Kissinger's Bluff" turned out to be one of those over-the-weekend assignments. Since New York's covers sometimes poke an extra finger in the ribs of the cover stories' victims, design director Milton Glaser, editorial director Byron Dobell and Bernard had pictured Kissinger as having his bluff called in the card game of international negotiation.

The sketch was handed over to Hess on a Friday night; film had to be at the engraver no later than Tuesday morning. Even so, Hess turned in a stylized piece of finished art, meticulously detailed down to the pearls of sweat on Kissinger's forehead and the pinstripes on his suit.

Budget for this job was the standard $500 cover fee. Production—four-color separations—was standard as well.

The cover for "You Oughta Be in Pictures," on the other hand, was completed by artist Burt Silverman in two weeks, but the circumstances surrounding the assignment

New York's New Divorce Bill: A Splitting Headache
Hanging Out With the Guru, by Sally Kempton
Bad News Coming for the 'Times,' by Chris Welles

75 CENTS   APRIL 12, 1976

NEW YORK

Calling Kissinger's Bluff
The Great Negotiator as A Loser
By Aaron Latham

were also rather unusual.

New York's year-end issue was to be based around movies in New York—the story of filmmaking on the East Coast from the early days on Long Island to sophisticated location techniques of the '70s. As it was a special issue, Bernard notes that they wanted it to look visually different from the regular format.

Originally, Bernard had discussed with contributing artist Ed Sorel the possibility of doing one of his cartoon-and-comment spots. In the meantime, Sorel had come across a picture of silent screen heroine Clara Bow and suggested that it would work perfectly for the cover; but he didn't see doing it himself. Other cover ideas were tried and scrapped as everybody kept coming back to Sorel's; the nostalgic quality seemed the most appropriate. Finally, Sorel recommended using Silverman, who did a pastel drawing in the same style as the earlier work.

According to Bernard, this was one of the year's largest selling issues. It is also interesting to see how well suited the New York logo is to the dated style of the visual—an amazingly flexible design.—*VFB*

Special Year-end Movie Issue

Your Pull-out Map of the Stars
Ed Sorel's Coming Attractions—Watch Out!
How They Make Movies in New York

75 CENTS

New York

DEC. 29, 1975/JAN. 5, 1976

You Oughta Be In Pictures
Scenes From New York's Love Affair With the Movies

Publisher: New York Magazine
Kissinger:
Art directors/designers: Milton Glaser, Walter Bernard
Illustrator: Richard Hess
Pictures:
Art directors: Milton Glaser, Walter Bernard
Designers: Milton Glaser, Walter Bernard, Ed Sorel
Illustrator: Burt Silverman

One afternoon, Bobby Womack, songwriter and singer, was driving on a Los Angeles freeway with his new record producer, David Robinson. Apropos of nothing in particular, Womack, wishing to express his satisfaction over Robinson's approach to his music, said he felt like he was standing in a safety zone. Whereupon both men said, ''That's it,'' realizing that the perfect title for Womack's upcoming album had been found.

When it came time to illustrate the album cover, though, Womack wanted more than a literal approach. His interpretation of the concept of ''safety zone'' had grown to encompass the sense of security created by one person for another, especially the parent-child aspect. Any kind of street scene shot, then, would prove unsatisfying.

Designer Ria Lewerke started fairly early in the recording schedule to derive her layouts from Womack's theme. While the action of the cover had to play off the concept in a more abstract manner than had been done before, she wanted to retain the overall graphic quality she had given Womack's earlier covers. Type must be subtle, with the letters of Womack's name widely spaced, and the album title placed on the cover in an almost offhand manner. The picture itself would be placed within a border.

Lewerke presented Womack with three layouts depicting him playing with his son, and Womack, fortunately,

Above: album front. Left: inside sleeve. Opposite: album back.

selected the one which she and photographer Moshe Brakha liked the best.

Brakha's shots, which were used for the back cover and the inner sleeve as well, create the intimate mood Womack was searching for without being corny. While they are a refreshing change from the ultra-cool ''personality'' covers usually associated with Womack's past albums, it is interesting to note that the car the Womacks are playing in is a Rolls Royce, another sort of safety zone entirely.

Lewerke notes that it took five separations to obtain the quality of the original art. The entire project took five weeks.—*VFB*

Client: United Artists Records
Design firm: United Artists Records Art Department, Hollywood
Designer/art director: Ria Lewerke
Photographer: Moshe Brakha
Letterer/type designer: Composition Arts

The Songs:
Daylight
Everything's Gonna Be Alright
I Feel A Groove Comin' On
I Wish It Would Rain
Love Ain't Something You Can Get For Free
Something You Got
Trust In Me
Where There's A Will, There's A Way

Produced by David Robinson & Friends, Inc.

The legendary little old lady in Dubuque, for whom the New Yorker was decidedly not edited, but who likely wielded considerable influence on the design of Saturday Evening Post covers, clearly has not been invited to participate in the deliberations involving choice of cover illustrations for National Lampoon. Secure in the open-mindedness of its readership, the Lampoon is free to satirize anything and everything. If the joke just happens to include some sexual connotation, it only makes sense for the cover design to capitalize on that with its own prurient pictorial observation.

For the March 1976 issue, art director Peter Kleinman asked illustrator Rick Meyerowitz to translate the cover title, "In Like a Lion," into a visual pun. The idea had been conceived at a monthly board meeting and Meyerowitz was an obvious choice for the job. "He is great at making obscene animal rituals look almost cute—and sellable in supermarkets," Kleinman explains. Even if the budget had been 50 times more than it was ($1000, including color separations), Kleinman feels that Meyerowitz would have handled his solution the same way. Reaction to the design was generally enthusiastic. Only the distributors balked.

Editor Sean Kelly had the idea for the cover of the April 1976 Lampoon, an issue devoted to sports. "We had to say sports without showing physical competition, and be funny at the same time,"

March Issue
In Like a Lion

Monty Python Parody   Snuff Porn Flick   Free New York City Municipal Bond

NATIONAL LAMPOON

IND 34490

March 1976

Price $1.00

Kleinman recalls. The Olympics made a good focal point and the obvious target for satire was the controversy about transsexual athletes. "Chris Callis did the shot," says Kleinman; "all I did was stuff the model's crotch and say 'hold still.'" With only one week in which to come up with an idea, find a model, arrange the shooting, complete the mechanical and make separations, Kleinman was unable to insist on the kind of perfection he wanted in the final printing. He feels that the background gray should have been lightened, the red in the skin tones increased, and the word "sports" etched for a better fit behind the model's legs.

Publisher: National Lampoon
Art director/designer: Peter Kleinman
March 1976:
Illustrator: Rick Meyerowitz
April 1976:
Photographer: Chris Callis

Art Direction

A publication for the design trade can indulge in the sophisticated use of pure design without risking the alienation of its readers or a falling off of circulation. With his cover for the February 1976 issue of Art Direction, designer Mike Salisbury has taken full advantage of this opportunity. His design is truly art for art's sake, or perhaps it would be more appropriate to say pop-art for art's sake.

Fascinated by the visual impact of a 75¢ plastic mask, a mass-produced toy derived from costumes used in a popular Japanese science-fiction TV series, Salisbury decided it should be shared with the design community. "This mask is part of a whole merchandising phenomenon in Japan," he reports, "and in my opinion, represents some of the best current toy and packaging design." The addition of a pencil to the lips gives the face the appearance of a pensive art director. Cropped in and enlarged, the visual elements become abstract. "I knew before I photographed this cover, I'd like it," Salisbury observes, adding candidly, "this is unusual, knowing how insecure we may be from time to time with our work."

Publisher: Art Direction
Art director: Stanley Stellar
Designer: Mike Salisbury

A Charming Field for an Encounter

As part of its official celebration of the Bicentennial, the U.S. National Park Service, a division of the Department of the Interior, has undertaken an ambitious but extremely worthwhile publishing program. To commemorate the history of every major Revolutionary War battle site in America, the service plans to issue a series of illustrated booklets and posters. The project, begun in 1976, is expected to last another eight years.

While considering one of the first publications in the series, art director Nick Kirilloff, on the recommendation of an anonymous benefactor (no one can recall who made the suggestion), asked illustrator Daniel Maffia for samples of his work. Subsequently, Maffia was given the job of doing a cover and interior illustrations for *A Charming Field for an Encounter,* a booklet about Fort Necessity battlefield where George Washington, then an untried colonel in his early twenties, fought the opening battle of the French and Indian War. Maffia attacked the problem enthusiastically, went on location in Pennsylvania "just to get the feel of the land," and rented an authentic costume from Brooks-Van Horn to insure the accuracy of his illustration. For his portrayal of Washington, he got as close to the original source as possible, an early portrait—the only one of Washington from that period—by the American painter Charles Willson Peale. "Since I wanted it to be historically correct," Maffia remarks, "I copied it more or less exactly."

The Park Service was so pleased with Maffia's cover that they decided to duplicate it as a poster. The original art (approximately 9″ by 12″) was blown up and Kirilloff handled the typography. "The people in charge of government publications felt that the fort should be added at the bottom of the original art," recalls Maffia, whose fee was not increased to cover the use of his illustration as a poster, "but thanks to Kirilloff's good taste and judgment, his superiors were persuaded to leave everything as it was. All he did was add a green border." Maffia likes the reproduced version better than his original.

Client: National Park Service, U.S. Department of the Interior
Art director/designer: Nick Kirilloff
Illustrator: Daniel Maffia

Above: booklet cover. Right: poster based on original cover art.

A handsome paperback that could easily hold its own on the shelves of any retail book store, this cover is one of a series of 12 remedial readers used to teach public high school students who have fallen behind in their grade reading level. The series, which includes fiction, non-fiction and poetry, was designed over a period of three-and-a-half months as an in-house assignment. Carefully chosen cover illustrations are framed in a variety of bright colors which give each book a cheerful individuality and make the entire series an attractive, colorful unit. Although these texts are marketed at conventions and sold through education adoption committees to public school systems throughout the U.S. and Canada, art director William Mathison feels that the heaviest initial impact is in the cover and that the artwork is, consequently, an influential factor in the sale of the book.

The story of *Junkyard Holiday* centers around the activities of two young boys who go to visit their uncle. He lives in a dilapidated house in the middle of a junkyard where the boys discover an old Rolls Royce which they refurbish and enter in an antique car show. "The first sketches were rejected," Mathison explains, "because the emphasis on the junkyard hit the viewer with a depression image which was too heavy for the light, somewhat humorous story." In the final version, the elegant car was given

prominence with the junkyard relegated to the background. The resulting composite, a photograph printed in sepia with background color showing through the drop-out areas, was more appropriate to the text. "It meshed in nicely with the other books in the series," Mathison comments, "and has a contemporary quality which is important to the students using this material."

Publisher: The Economy Co.
Art director/illustrator: William Mathison
Designer: Paul Cornett
Photographer: Connie Hwang

Opposite page: final cover. Above: preliminary sketches. The first idea was rejected because too much emphasis was placed on the junkyard, the second because more than one car was given prominence. The third sketch, showing a new and final title, was accepted. Below: four other covers in series.

Art director Steve Phillips thinks of the New Times audience as youngish, liberal, educated people and he likes to give them something to think about. One of his more humorous assignments was the cover of an issue headlining Barbra Streisand's fling with a Beverly Hills hairdresser whose influence over the superstar's life began when he styled a wig for her and has developed to such an extent that he is now the producer of her latest movie. Struck by the sheer absurdity of the situation, Phillips asked illustrator Bill Nelson to do an illustration that would make her look a little silly. He felt that the likeness should be a good one but not too serious. The emperor's-new-clothes imagery suggested by Streisand's bald head was unintended.

A much more serious treatment was required for the cover of an issue featuring an article questioning the investigation into the assassination of John F. Kennedy. To get the maximum reaction to a subject that needed attention, Phillips made use of a violent, repellent image. Dickran Palulian's illustration is realistic but contemporary, like the blow-up of a motion picture frame, a stop-action image that shocks and disgusts the viewer. ''This is probably the only time in my career that I pushed what I knew to be in bad taste,'' Phillips comments. ''I felt strongly about the subject and tried to picture a horrible event in an appropriate manner. No covering up on

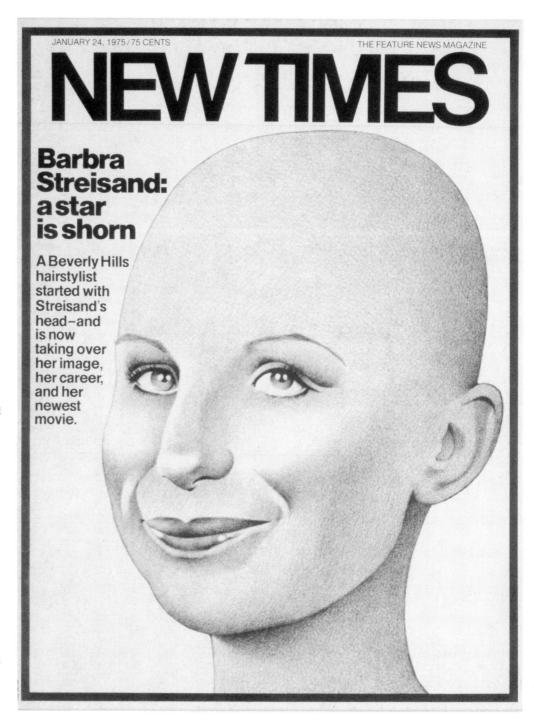

the assassination—no covering up on the cover.'' In three years of publication, this was New Time's best-selling issue.

Publisher: New Times
Art director/designer:
Steve Phillips
Illustrators: Bill Nelson
(''Streisand''), Dickran Palulian
(''JFK'')

Carly Simon
Playing Possum

Creating the sleeve for Carly Simon's record album didn't start with the familiar conference-table concept meeting. In fact, the project actually began with Simon expressing to art director Glen Christensen her desire to work with photographer Norman Seeff.

Simon's interest in Seeff stemmed from his unique, controversial camera treatment of rock superstars. Rather than pose them or even take candid shots, Seeff asks his subjects to ''give me you for these pictures'' and treats the shooting session as an emotionally based relationship for him to record. It has been argued that by allowing his subjects such enormous latitude, Seeff doesn't fulfill his creative obligations, and that the emotional strain of being themselves is more than some performers can handle; nevertheless Seeff's technique has earned a reputation among music and communications people as one which must be experienced.

Early in the recording schedule (allowing two to three months for completion of the album cover), Simon's initial session with Seeff took place. Seeff shot the singer wearing her black negligee in both black-and-white and color. What followed was an attempt at selecting the album's front cover photograph.

For a week Seeff, Simon, her manager, Arlyne Rothberg, and Christensen caucused over the pictures, each of them making

Client: Electra Records
Art director: Glen Christensen
Colors: Two blacks, greenish-brown
Cover:
Designer/photographer:
Norman Seeff
Printer: Album Graphics
Poster:
Designers: Glen Christensen,
Norman Seeff
Printer: Westland Graphics
Size: 24″ by 36″ each

selections. The outcome was their agreement that a second session was needed. Seeff photographed Simon again with different lighting and wardrobe. Then came another week of comparing the two sessions.

Finally, "everyone started to swing back to the first session," Christensen notes. "Our diversity was galvanized when Seeff honed in on the shot that became the cover. The rest just fell into place—picking the back cover and inner sleeve." The title was lifted from one of the songs on the album; it also neatly works in with the mood of the cover shot.

Although the original plan was to use four-color process, Christensen found, after making separations and color corrections, that the quality and mood of the originals was disappearing. He then had the job completely reseparated as a duograph in greenish brown and black with a second black pass by a high-contrast plate to extend the range and depth of the shadow areas. Christensen felt that this held the impact of the originals and insured a powerful finished product.

It was so powerful, in fact,

that after Elektra's marketing group saw the album, it was decided to produce posters of both the front and back covers. (The back cover image also became the focal point of a promotional billboard that Christensen designed for location on the Sunset Strip.) While Elektra's album posters tend toward close adaptations of front covers to secure quick identification among record store patrons, it is unusual to reproduce back cover images as well.

In designing the posters, Christensen found that the front cover cropped best as a vertical, the back as a horizontal; to have worked both vertically would have meant cropping out Simon's leg, destroying the desired effect.

Perhaps the most exciting aspect of this project was the element of risk involved in using a radically unstructured shooting-session technique and the cohesive, successful pieces that came as a result.—VFB

Opposite page: album front. Right: poster based on album front. Below: poster based on album back.

At least once each year, the Master Eagle Gallery holds an exhibit of work done by students in the Media Arts Department at the School of Visual Arts. The spring, 1975, exhibition was called ''Double Take'' and consisted of an ingenious collection of original works of art aimed at proving to an unsuspecting public that people don't see what is actually before them. ''The idea behind 'Double Take,' '' explains Media Arts co-chairman Richard Wilde, ''was that people react to familiar images in a mechanical way, not really seeing what is there but seeing what they *think* should be there.'' The poster announcing the show did so in a manner guaranteed to involve viewers in a double-take experience before they ever set foot in the gallery. Based on Grant Wood's painting, ''American Gothic,'' the illustration seems at first glance merely a copy of that famous picture. Further scrutiny reveals, however, that the farmer and his wife have switched heads. The show included paintings, drawings, and three-dimensional art as well as a live person in a *trompe-l'oeil* setting. ''He portrayed the wax figure of a fortune-teller,'' Wilde confides, ''but was able to participate in the exhibit only on opening night.'' The entire experience gave students and department chairmen a chance to make some interesting observations about the reactions of the audience. ''When people couldn't see the things that were wrong, it

The School of Visual Arts Presents
Double Take
An exhibition at The Master Eagle Gallery, 40 West 25th Street, 6th Floor, April 21 through May 20. From 10 A.M. to 4 P.M., Monday through Friday. The exhibition will include students work in illustration and graphic design.

The School of Visual Arts in cooperation with The Master Eagle Family of Companies

Double Take

The Master Eagle Family of Companies invites you to the opening of ''Double Take'' an exhibition by the School of Visual Arts
April 17, 1975, 5:00 P.M. to 8:00 P.M.
The Master Eagle Gallery, 6th Floor, 40 West 25th St., New York, N.Y.

Admission by ticket only   Cocktails and refreshments

Client: School of Visual Arts
Art director/designer: Richard Wilde
Illustrator: Judi Mintzer
Copywriter: Dee Ito
Printer: Master Eagle Family of Companies
Colors: Full color
Size: 21″ by 32″

Top: poster announcing show. Left: invitation to opening. Above: admission ticket.

made them very nervous,'' Wilde recalls; ''but the ones who realized that they had made a mistake and admitted it enjoyed the show a lot.''

Not quite a year later, Master Eagle sponsored another show of SVA students' work, developed, appropriately enough, around a Bicentennial theme. Entitled ''America: My Country 'Tis of Thee,'' the exhibit contained an unusually large number of original and printed pieces including full-color postage stamps, large portraits of famous Americans, and sculpture. To publicize this comprehensive collection of visual statements about America and draw attendance to the exhibition, Wilde wanted a poster that would symbolize the students' thoughts and feelings about their country. Elaborating on the drawing of an ice cream cone by Takao Matsumoto, Wilde decided that a three-dimensional cone would make a more powerful image and asked Chris Bobbin to make one. Using clear vinyl, which she stuffed, painted, and sewed together, Bobbin created a sculpture which was actually only about half the size of the cone on the poster. ''The medium itself made a statement about the country,'' Wilde explains, ''and the image could be taken as either a positive or negative comment.'' The headline, hand-lettered by Tetsuya Matsuura, is a neon sign that never goes out. The construction was photographed against a black background, necessitating an additional printing of the black plate to prevent overlap and define the edge of the cone.

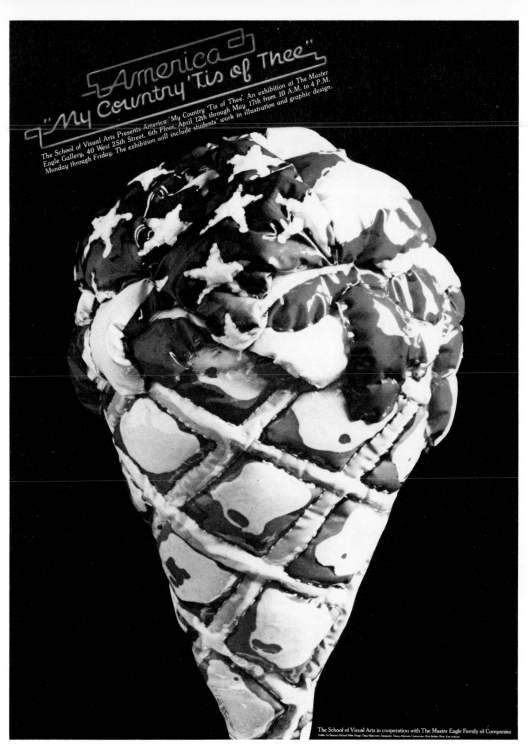

Client: School of Visual Arts
Art director: Richard Wilde
Designers: Takao Matsumoto, Tetsuya Matsuura, Richard Wilde
Illustrator: Chris Bobbin
Photographer: Ken Ambrose
Lettering: Tetsuya Matsuura
Printer: Master Eagle Family of Companies
Colors: Full color
Size: 23″ by 33″

Above: poster announcing show.
Left: sketches for original painting of ice cream cone.

Baltimore Experimental High School

The Baltimore Experimental High School is a unique private institution accredited by the Board of Education. The staff is committed to an all-encompassing program of learning rather than schooling in the traditional sense of the word, and includes volunteers as well as paid teachers. The students, accepted from all levels of society regardless of whether or not they can pay the tuition, plan their own curricula, share in making policy decisions, and help with the school's administration and maintenance. Although the school's operations are partially funded by grants, additional revenues must constantly be solicited from private individuals and charitable organizations to help cover the costs of scholarships, salaries, educational supplies, and building renovations. For this reason, BEHS issues a considerable quantity of promotional fund-raising material, all of it produced within a minimal budget, usually by designers and staff members who do not charge for their services.

Peter Traynor's design for one such brochure is an elaborate fold-out which opens up into a poster showing the school building as a butterfly in flight. "I thought it would be nice to give something to those you are asking of," says Traynor, "so I did a brochure that dismantles into a gift." Influenced by a winter-festival poster created by Traynor's associate, Dave Franek, with whom he had formerly taught a graphic design course at the school, the mailing piece makes use of an enlarged halftone dot pattern and the butterfly which he and Franek consider an ideal symbol for BEHS. "The school is a radical education system," Franek explains. "Students who come from traditional schools go through a transition there. It's as if they learned to release their dormant talents, spread their wings and fly away." Traynor showed his sketches to the client as a courtesy ("If it's possible to give you more than 100 per cent freedom, these people do it," he reports) and once they were approved, undertook to have the finished brochure produced as inexpensively as possible.

His first task was to convince a small, black-only, quick-job printer with an 11" by 17" offset press that he could handle a full-size brochure to be printed both sides on light blue paper in two colors—burgundy and dark blue. This accomplished, he recruited a group of students to hand-bind the folders with string. "It's as much a learning experience as anything else," explains Traynor, who says that he

has been able to produce some fairly exotic designs for the school simply because he can rely on the free labor of a student production staff willing to do anything that will benefit their alma mater. In this case, the students gathered in someone's living room folding and binding until the job was done. "I wouldn't say it was exactly a party," Traynor recalls, "but it wasn't a serious work detail either."

The poster, which was delivered exactly one week after Traynor began thinking about it, has been enthusiastically received, reprinted once, and seems destined for a long and useful life.

Client: Baltimore Experimental High School
Art director/designer/ illustrator: Peter Traynor
Photographer: Richard Anderson
Copywriter: Howie Evans
Printer: The Printer's Devil
Colors: Burgundy and dark blue on light blue stock
Size: 5½" by 8½" folded; 11" by 17" open

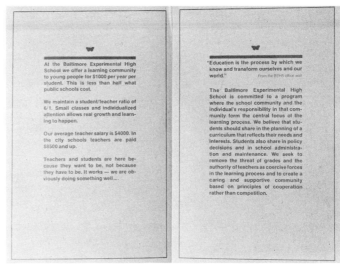

Opposite page: all three sections of brochure opened up. Above: Franek's poster which inspired Traynor to use butterfly motif. Right: spreads from brochure. Below: butterfly illustration.

Other than designing a cover for a graphic arts trade magazine, there is probably no assignment that offers an artist fewer limitations than producing a poster for an exhibition of graphic design. Directed at a sympathetic, often professional audience and usually concerned with publicizing an event that appeals to the trade, it gives the designer a chance to satisfy his own creative inclinations without the risk of producing something too personal or too avant-garde to be understood.

In two different posters announcing events having to do with graphic design, Takenobu Igarashi has taken advantage of these attractive circumstances to play with graphic elements which have a special fascination for him. Perhaps because English is, for him, a foreign language whose written form differs greatly from that of his own native tongue, Igarashi became interested in making three-dimensional images based on the letterforms of the Roman alphabet. Intrigued by the abstract qualities of lettershapes which have been transformed into solid structural motifs, he·has created two designs which produce dissimilar visual effects even though they are based on the same graphic concept.

For a poster publicizing a special issue of the Japanese design magazine Idea, devoted to a survey of graphic designers on the West Coast, Igarashi has used his three-dimensional letters as a kind of modern version of the

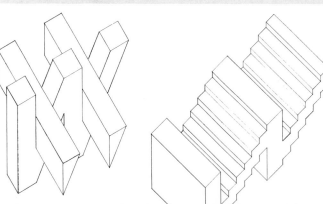

Publisher: Idea Magazine
Art director/designer:
Takenobu Igarashi
Printer: Light Printing Co.
Colors: Yellow, coral, pink/purple, blue/purple, brown
Size: 28¾″ by 40⅝″

Left and opposite page: sketches for three-dimensional letter W.

illustrated initials in illuminated manuscripts of the early Renaissance. Each letter heads a list of designers whose last names begin with it. Deployed in an attractive, colorful overall pattern, the letters also serve to indicate that the designers are Western rather than Japanese.

Igarashi's entry in the international poster exhibition, "Graphic Design Now," at Tokyo's Seibu Museum of Art, reproduces the three-dimensional forms with entirely different results. Because Igarashi was teaching at UCLA when he was invited to participate in the exhibition, he decided to illustrate his poster with those initials. Bigger, more complicated, and painted in more vibrant colors than the letterforms on his Idea poster, the three-dimensional UCLA, with its steps, columns and multi-faceted structural elements, suggests the architectural complex of a university campus.

UNIVERSITY OF CALIFORNIA, LOS ANGELES

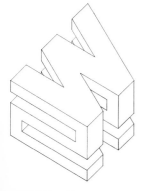
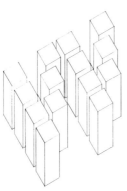
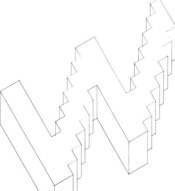

Client/art director/designer: Takenobu Igarashi
Printer: Light Printing Co.
Colors: Brown, purple, green, yellow, red-orange, black, beige
Size: 28¾″ by 40⅝″

To illustrate the poster announcing her one-woman exhibition of drawings, paintings and collages, Heather Cooper chose a meticulously detailed oil painting reminiscent in certain respects of pictures from the Italian Renaissance. A graceful figure with Botticelliesque hair and brocaded dress stands against a distant landscape. Ferns, flowers and the delicate tendrils of a vine, drawn with the same scrupulous regard for accuracy one might find in a botany primer, curl about her flowing skirt. Even the colors—muted greens, blues and grays—suggest the mystery and romance of a long lost time. The headline and supplemental copy, set in a classic serif face, give the announcement a bookish quality appropriate for a show called "The Art of the Illustrator."

An excellent example of Cooper's imaginative, precise style, the poster serves as well to suggest the elegance of the exhibition itself, which was sponsored by the Abitibi Paper Company and held in the lobby gallery of First Canadian Place, a new Toronto office building. Proceeds from the sale of original art and reproductions of Cooper's work were donated to a special scholarship for a student of illustration.

Client: Abitibi Paper Co.
Design firm: Burns, Cooper, Donoahue, Fleming & Co. Ltd., Toronto
Art director: Robert Burns
Designer: Jim Donoahue
Illustrator: Heather Cooper
Printer: Herzig Somerville Ltd.
Colors: Full color
Size: 20½ " by 39 "

Danish Housing

When the University of California at Berkeley needed a poster to announce a forthcoming lecture on Danish housing by an architect from Copenhagen, designer Marc Treib received the standard college dictum: keep it cheap. The talk, sponsored by the Department of Architecture, was open to the whole university but its audience would be drawn primarily from the departments of architecture, land architecture, and city planning, all of which are housed in the same building. Treib is no stranger to low-budget assignments, and undismayed by the prospect of another, he decided that the best approach was to have fun. "I could take great liberty with the subject matter since it was all 'in house,'" he explains, "and in this case I knew that the speaker had a sense of humor."

Treib, who says that he starts with time and money and works back from that, first considered planning his design around a picture of the Danish flag. The budget limited him to using the diazo printing process, however, and diazo restricted his choice of color to black or brown. Rejecting flag-waving for a more subtle kind of patriotism, he finally settled on a visual pun emphasizing the most characteristic attributes of a Danish pastry, its sugary glaze and swirling shape. But his original pencil drawing couldn't be reproduced in halftone because it was too expensive. Although Treib felt that the gloss and roundness couldn't be so realistically depicted in line, he decided that people would look at the title after the drawing, then reconsider the drawing and see the joke. "The irony," he points out cheerfully, "is that in Denmark and most of Europe a 'Danish' is called 'Wienerbrod' and would be more appropriate for a lecture on Viennese housing. But in America, it makes sense."

The job was completed in one week at a total cost of $27 for the initial run of 40 posters. The popularity of the design was undisputed. Treib reports that "more than the usual number were stolen."

Client: Department of Architecture, University of California, Berkeley
Designer/Illustrator: Marc Treib
Printer: Berkeley Blueprint Co.
Color: Brown-line diazo
Size: 18" by 24"

Below: line drawing from original sketch.

Otto Piene

When Jacqueline Casey was given the task of designing a poster to publicize an exhibition of paintings and drawings by Otto Piene, she decided to use one of his own works of art as an illustration. After discussing several possibilities with the artist, she chose a startling, textured gouache because she felt it would make the most successful reproduction. Entitled "The Black, the Fire and the Flower," the painting itself became the poster—its fiery red background silhouetting Piene's name, then smoldering away to a charred and blackened abstraction.

The exhibition was sponsored by the MIT Committee on the Visual Arts, and the poster, which was displayed on bulletin boards, in the halls of university buildings, and in art galleries, was also produced folded and used as a mailer. Its size was determined not only by the dimensions of the original work of art, but also by the 1-ounce limitation for first-class postage. "The announcement was popular," Casey sums up. "The artist and I were both satisfied with the reproduction of his work."

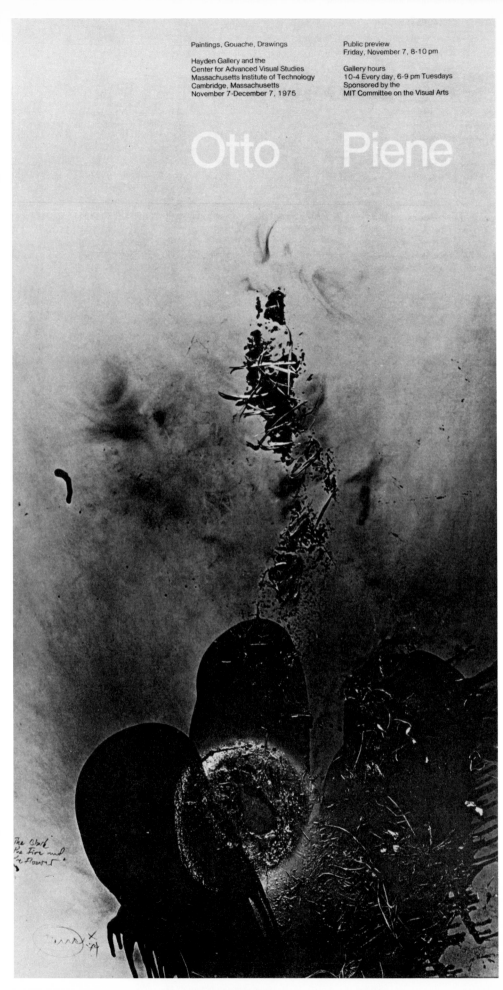

Paintings, Gouache, Drawings

Hayden Gallery and the
Center for Advanced Visual Studies
Massachusetts Institute of Technology
Cambridge, Massachusetts
November 7-December 7, 1975

Public preview
Friday, November 7, 8-10 pm

Gallery hours
10-4 Every day, 6-9 pm Tuesdays
Sponsored by the
MIT Committee on the Visual Arts

Otto Piene

Client: MIT Committee on the Visual Arts
Design firm: MIT Design Services, Cambridge, MA
Art director/designer: Jacqueline S. Casey
Photographer: Nishan Bichajian
Printer: Rapid Service Press
Colors: Full color
Size: 17″ by 33″

We the People

In observance of the Bicentennial celebration, the National Museum of History and Technology in Washington, D.C., a subsidiary of the Smithsonian Institution, installed a large permanent exhibit called "We the People." Funded by a special grant from Congress, the exhibit, which was designed by Robert Staples and Barbara Fahs Charles, is devoted to an examination of the American people and their government. Consisting of official documents, art objects, and political memorabilia, the collection is arranged in three sections based on Lincoln's words from the Gettysburg Address, "government of the people, by the people and for the people." In the first section, a variety of national symbols are displayed; the second section provides a visual history of American rights and political processes; and the final section defines the government's obligations to its citizens.

Although funds were eventually allocated for an official poster advertising the exhibit, there was a period during which the museum directors felt that an announcement of that sort was one thing they would have to eliminate from what seemed to be a very tight budget. Staples and Charles, who were pleased with the installation and anxious to let their friends and clients know about it, decided to produce a poster on their own which would serve not only as publicity for the exhibit, but also as a promotion piece for their design firm.

With only three weeks left before the show opened and their own budget problems to consider, Staples and Charles agreed to use line artwork and reproduce the poster in black diazo. They selected for the illustration a fabric Uncle Sam doll which belongs to them but is on loan to the exhibition. The work of a turn-of-the-century toy designer named Palmer Cox,

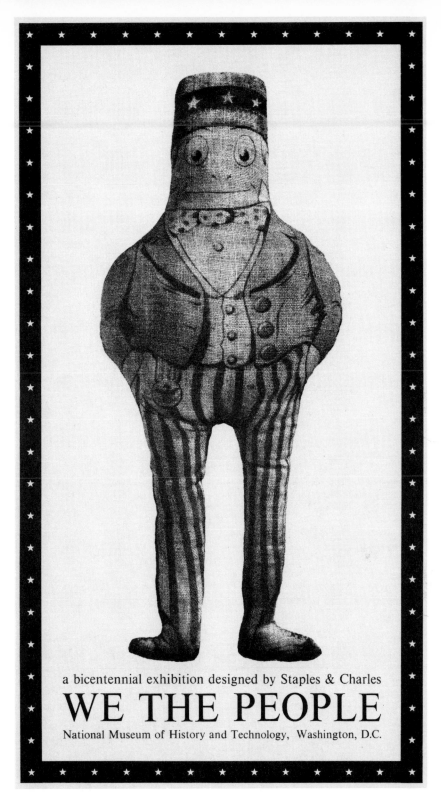

a bicentennial exhibition designed by Staples & Charles

WE THE PEOPLE

National Museum of History and Technology, Washington, D.C.

the figure is displayed in the show as a patriotic symbol and made an ideal image for the poster. Working with a mezzotint of the doll forthrightly displayed above the headline, Staples and Charles repeated the starry pattern from his headband as a decorative border motif. The poster was printed in an edition of 100.

Client/design firm: Staples & Charles, Washington, D.C.
Designers: Robert Staples, Barbara Fahs Charles
Photographer: Rick Steadry
Printer: Exspeedite Blueprint Service, Inc.
Color: Black diazo
Size: 18½" by 34"

Sand Dunes

In 1972, the education officer at the British Museum decided to publish a series of posters illustrating plants in their natural settings. Designated Plant Ecology Wall-Charts, the posters, which will number 15 in all, are sold by catalog and through the museum shop to high schools, colleges and amateur naturalists. The charts are intended to provide an easy means of recognition for some of the more common British wildflowers and plants, and although the series includes, at this writing, 10 attractive finished charts describing a variety of environments such as chalk grasslands, meadows, hedgerows and salt marshes, Sand Dunes is the only one chosen for publication in this Casebook.

Illustrated with colorful charm and scrupulous accuracy by Barbara Nicholson, who was commissioned to do the entire series, Sand Dunes, like the other charts, is the end product of a long and unusually exacting production process. An experienced botanical artist best-known in the U.S. for illustrating several volumes in a series of books on botany published by the Oxford University Press, Nicholson undertakes each assignment with extraordinary care and meticulous attention to detail. "She takes about six weeks to do the actual painting, but she does a great deal of research before this," relates C.J.Owen of the British Museum. "She makes a point of painting each plant fresh even though she might have painted it a dozen times before. For this reason she will often delay a whole painting while waiting for one flower to come into bloom. This research can take several months depending on the locality because she often travels to a particular habitat to see the plants *in situ*." After the illustrations are finished, each drawing is inspected by the appropriate expert in the museum's botany department to insure that the highest scientific standards are maintained. "But," Owen adds, "Ms. Nicholson's knowledge of botany is such that only the most minor adjustments are usually necessary." The final painting is done in gouache on cardboard.

The posters are printed in five colors and usually require two sets of proofs before Owen and his associates are satisfied with the accuracy of the reproduction. The total budget for each chart is approximately $2000.

The series has been so well received that the charts were reprinted within 18 months of their publication in 1973 and were reprinted again in 1976. A total of 40,000 copies of Sand Dunes has been issued so far.

Client: British Museum (Natural History)
Illustrator: Barbara Nicholson
Editor: C. J. Owen
Printer: Mears, Caldwell Hacker
Distributed by: United Communications
Colors: Full color
Size: 24" by 31"

BYU Chamber Orchestra

Universities often form the body of many a rock band's touring schedule. Frequently, in fact, it takes little more than a radio announcement or even word-of-mouth to provide sell-outs at the campus auditorium. Classical music, on the other hand, while having its loyal coterie (usually among music majors), isn't likely to have such widespread popularity; the twin-bladed stigma of stuffy and boring is difficult to erase. As a result, more elaborate means for spreading the word are often necessary when an orchestra is scheduled to appear.

McRay Magleby faced just this difficulty when he was assigned to design a poster announcing Brigham Young University Chamber Orchestra's next performance. His "psychedelic" treatment of baroque musicians, complete with Dayglo color, certainly proves that getting high on one's own sounds isn't limited to rock stars.

Working with a severely restrictive budget of $200 and a size limitation imposed by campus bulletin boards, Magleby planned his design for the silkscreen process: flat Dayglo color, bold lines, no close registration. The budget only allowed for three colors but Magleby made full use of it by overlapping blue and orange, achieving brown.

The orchestra director, who had liked Magleby's initial design, requested more figures, so several were added drifting off the edges.

Of the 300 posters printed, 25 were distributed. Space for information was deliberately left open and is filled in by hand for each performance. Perhaps the best part about the poster, though, and indicative of its success, is that it created an identity for the chamber ensemble. Each time the floating orchestra appears, it's automatically understood that a concert is coming up.—*VFB*

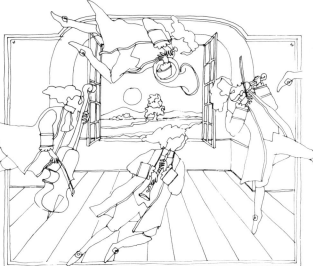

Client: Brigham Young University Music Department
Design firm: Graphic Communications, Brigham Young University, Provo, UT
Art director/designer/ illustrator/copywriter: McRay Magleby
Printer: Graphic Communications, Brigham Young University
Colors: Blue and orange Dayglo silkscreen ink
Size: 20″ by 16″

Born a Loser/
My Mommy Is Sick

One of the most exciting courses at the School of Visual Arts is Public Advertising System. A unique portfolio class for third- and fourth-year students, it was developed in the early '70s when the school's administration noticed a growing lack of enthusiasm among upperclassmen for the study of advertising. Partly to furnish the students with more exciting assignments and the chance to work with people outside the school, but more significantly, to help answer what media arts director Richard Wilde calls the moral question—whether studying advertising means selling out—Wilde and instructor Frank Young decided to organize a class which could work as a creative team on real assignments. Local non-profit organizations were solicited as clients and PAS went into operation offering a full range of skilled services from concept to final printing.

One of PAS's recent assignments was a poster for the New York City Health Department. Designed to encourage expectant mothers to prevent retardation in newborns by seeking regular prenatal checkups, the poster, titled "Born a Loser," was displayed on the street, in store windows, in clinics, and in high school counseling offices. Art directors Frank Young and Corinne Felder had originally planned to illustrate the poster with a traditional shot of mother and child. Close-ups of the baby made during the course of the shooting, however,

BORN A LOSER.

If you're pregnant and anemic your child may be born retarded.
It is important to see your doctor or
call the New York City Health Dept. 566-7711
The School of Visual Arts Public Advertising System

Client: New York City Prenatal Clinics
Design firm: School of Visual Arts/Public Advertising System, New York
Art Director: Corinne Felder
Designer/photographer: Frank Young
Colors: Black-and-white
Size: 17½" by 22"

seemed far more effective. Enlarged to fit the poster, the infant's head and eye—two times their normal size—became a powerful graphic image.

Another PAS design—a picture which seems at first glance to contradict its headline—gives prominence to the image of an older child. The idea for "My Mommy is Sick" was developed over a period of six class hours by seven students working under Wilde's direction. The first concept—a little girl in bed calling attention to child abuse—was approved immediately but expanded to include hospital props and background. Produced for the Staten Island chapter of the Society for the Prevention of Cruelty to Children, the poster featured a hot-line number to encourage calls for help from friends, neighbors, or even the abusers themselves.

Although the poster, which was displayed mainly in clinics on Staten Island, would make an excellent subway announcement, Wilde reports that the costs of exhibiting it there are prohibitive. "The space for something like this would be free," he notes, "but the labor to put it up is too expensive."

Client: Society for the Prevention of Cruelty to Children
Design firm: School of Visual Arts/Public Advertising System, New York
Art directors/designers: Karla Ricciardi, Lila Lewenthal, Sue Taube, Susan Feinman, Richard Wilde
Copywriters: Linda Williams, Terry Studer
Photographer: Ken Ambrose
Colors: Black-and-white
Size: 17″ by 22″

Joseph Papp, founder/ producer of the New York Shakespeare Festival, is well-known for the originality and excitement of his productions. It is admirably consistent that the posters advertising two recent Papp theater pieces display the same qualities. Designed and illustrated by Paul Davis, these announcements are part of a series which include 12 productions altogether. Art director Reinhold Schwenk, at Case & McGrath, suggested the posters, which represent something of a departure from previous Shakespeare Festival advertising, as an alternative to full-page black-and-white newspaper ads which can cost in the neighborhood of $15,000 and may draw replies from only 200 or 300 readers. "We figured it was a good thing for the New York market," he says. "The poster is around. It's constantly on view."

Schwenk admired Davis's work, particularly his dramatic portrait of Che Guevara of some years back, and showed a collection of his illustrations to Papp, who agreed that Davis should do the painting announcing the production of *Hamlet* starring Sam Waterston. "Since the poster usually has to be prepared before the production is underway," Schwenk explains, "we try to have the artist see the actors, meet with the directors and talk to the costume people. The thrust of this production was that there was a madness in the circumstances rather than the character. Hamlet was to

be played as a sane person responding to an insane situation." Davis's first sketch, which was really a finished painting rather than a rough draft, is the one that was finally approved, but not without a certain amount of trial-and-error. Papp liked the original but thought it was too political. Davis's Hamlet, a powerful masculine figure against a fiery red background, whose angry expression resembles that of the rabble-rousing revolutionary figures in propaganda posters, was not the Hamlet that Papp wanted. Davis obligingly painted a more traditional character, but it was somehow too safe. "We all finally came to realize," Schwenk explains, "that something which unravels on the stage for two hours can't be expressed in its entirety in a single poster. The illustration can be somewhat interpretive using elements that come out of the play—but not too literal. A poster has to be a piece in itself." Once this decision was made, the rest of the series was much easier to produce.

Papp's production of *Three Penny Opera* sought to recreate the earthy, raw vulgarity of the original Berlin production. Although Davis was able to watch a rehearsal of the performance, he drew some of his inspiration from a German film of the play released during the 1930s. The final painting, a sinister, moody portrait of Mack the Knife, is based on a combination of subtle elements from both versions. "Davis gets inspired by little

things," Schwenk observes, "like the shadow of Macheath's hat on Raul Julia's face and the crude lettering on the signs the beggars carry in the movie."

Schwenk attributes the posters' success both to the powerful simplicity of Davis's style and to Papp, who, he reports, is not at all the usual client. A man who makes his decisions by himself without the red tape of committee discussions, he is also willing to break tradition. "On the Macheath poster, we cheated with the space," Schwenk explains, "and Papp didn't mind." Macheath's hand covers up the name of the theater and his hat partially obscures the title. The posters were originally displayed in subways, on station platforms and, in black-and-white, in New York newspapers. They were both subsequently reprinted for retail sales, and the *Three Penny Opera* illustration, which was mentioned in two drama reviews, has been converted for use on T-shirts.

Client: New York Shakespeare Festival
Art director/designer: Reinhold Schwenk
Illustrator/designer: Paul Davis
Printer: TDI
Colors: Full color
Size: 42" by 84"

Peugeot

When Peugeot's advertising agency, Delpire & Co., asked Seymour Chwast to design a series of three posters promoting motorcycle events in France, they gave him a little direction and a lot of opportunity to be as creative as he wished. The illustration was to have a traditional look reminiscent of the flat, decorative realism of poster art from the '20s and '30s. Aside from that, it was up to Chwast to translate the excitement of a race into visual symbols which would stir up the enthusiasm of a potential audience.

In this poster, his illustration suggests that the entire happening is a joy ride. The red and blue motorbike alone is a cheerful image, but the addition of circus performers takes it out of the ordinary world into a rarified atmosphere where every day is a holiday and no one has to go to work. The gay clothing and profiled one-dimensional figures do suggest the colorful simplicity of pre-World War II advertising. Even the copy recalls the calligraphic quality of hand-drawn sans-serif lettering typical of European posters done during that period.

Client: Peugeot
Design firm: Push Pin Studios, New York
Agency: Delpire & Co.
Designer/illustrator: Seymour Chwast
Colors: Full color
Size: 24″ by 31″

Another poster in the series.

Switzerland

The "Summer in Switzerland" program is a cooperative venture developed three years ago by J. Charles Walker, director of graphic design and illustration at Kent State University, and Armin Hoffman, head of graphic design at the Allgemeine Gewerbeschule in Basel. A combination study/travel workshop which may be taken for credit, the program gives students an opportunity to take courses with noted European designers and enjoy field trips throughout Switzerland and neighboring northern Italy.

To announce the 1975 session of the workshop to students of graphic design, Walker asked Glyphix to produce a poster which he could send to art schools throughout the U.S. "Glyphix," Walker explains, "is an honors program for Kent State art school students who are selected for the course by portfolio competition. It functions as a design and illustration service for the university—creating posters for summer programs in music and art, announcements for the chemistry department, and publications for WKSU-FM, the university radio network—and for outside, non-profit organizations as well." Although Glyphix does not charge for services, students receive credit for their work and clients must pay for materials. Walker is creative director of the studio.

Walker's summer workshop, which is not affiliated with the university, is self-supporting. The income from payments by students participating in the program covers all the bills, but his allowance for graphics and printing is limited. His instructions to Jeffrey Wilhelm, the graduate student whose job it was to design the poster, were simple: symbolize the idea of Swiss design, use only one color, and keep within a budget of $150. Wilhelm's solution, a carefully controlled arrangement of negative and positive space printed in red on a white background, is a typographic abstraction of the Swiss flag. Set in a restrained sans-serif face, the copy lists all information pertinent to the tour in four evenly balanced blocks whose flush margins form a white cross. Printed offset in an edition of 250, the poster elicited a gratifying number of inquiries and applications.

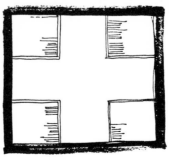

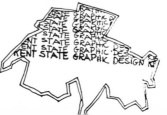

Client/art director/ copywriter: J. Charles Walker
Design firm: Glyphix, Kent, OH
Designer: Jeffrey Wilhelm
Printer: A&A Printing
Colors: Red on white
Size: 16" by 22"

Left: sketch and preliminary idea in which words are enclosed in the silhouette of a map of Switzerland.

Although the School of Visual Arts prints and exhibits a good deal of very professional looking student work, its subway posters are always designed by a member of the teaching staff. Displayed on New York's biggest bulletin board before a captive audience, the ads are produced to attract students interested in both degree and non-degree courses. Each season features a new campaign, which is usually planned to make use of a series of three or four provocative illustrations combined with one challenging headline.

Working with this year's copy, "Having Talent Isn't Worth Much Unless You Know What to Do with It," Richard Wilde asked Charles Lilly to do a painting for the third poster in the series. "It was a question of the artist taking the headline, finding the most powerful visual to illustrate it and at the same time making it a strong communication," Wilde remarks. Lilly, who chose to submit a number of ideas so that Wilde would have a selection, was not entirely satisfied with his original concept of the goose and her golden egg. "I thought it was too simple a design," he explains, "so I chose to make it more interesting and complicated by working up the surroundings." The intricate patterns of tangled grass and sunlight contrast effectively with the pale round shapes in the center, blurring at the lower edge to provide a uniform background for the type.

Having a talent isn't worth much unless you know what to do with it.

Degree and Non-Degree Programs. Day and Evening. Film, Photography, Media Arts (Advertising, Fashion, Illustration, Design), Fine Arts (Painting, Sculpture, Printmaking, Crafts), Video Tape, Dance, Humanities.

School of Visual Arts
209 East 23rd Street, New York, N.Y. 10010 679-7350

Client: School of Visual Arts
Art director: Silas H. Rhodes
Designer: Richard Wilde
Illustrator: Charles Lilly
Copywriter: Dee Ito
Colors: Full color
Size: 30" by 45"

Herman Miller Summer Picnic

Every summer, Herman Miller, Inc., designer and manufacturer of furniture, sponsors a picnic for the entire company. Two or three weeks beforehand, a poster publicizing the event is distributed throughout the Herman Miller administrative offices, manufacturing facilities, sales offices and showrooms. "Its obvious purpose is to announce the company picnic," explains graphic design director Stephen Frykholm, "but it actually functions as a corporate reference point. Both picnic and poster have become a tradition and people look forward to seeing what each new design will be like."

Colorful, festive close-ups of assorted all-American refreshments, Frykholm's designs can also be recognized as pure graphic abstractions. "In fact," he reports, "the posters are fun because initially many people do not see the image." Although Frykholm finds himself thinking about food ideas off and on throughout the year, he doesn't settle on any one of them until the picnic committee makes a final decision about the menu. To insure the accuracy of his 1975 design, "Cherry Pie," he worked closely from a "study model" which was subsequently devoured by his assistants.

When the first picnic poster was designed in 1970, Frykholm never dreamed that it would turn into an annual assignment. For that initial design, a close-up of yellow corn on the cob, white teeth, and red lips, Frykholm wanted large, flat, bright, glossy areas of color. Because the run was to be relatively small, he decided on screen printing to be financed by a supply budget. Since then, the program has become self-sustaining. Each summer, 500 posters are printed; 50 are used for announcing the picnic, and the balance are sold, the proceeds going to support the program.

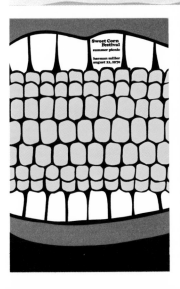

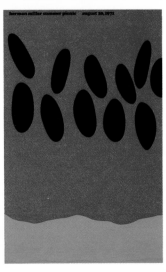

Client: Herman Miller, Inc.
Art director/designer: Stephen Frykholm
Printer: Continental Identification Products, Inc.
Colors: Specially mixed red, brown, beige and creme
Size: 25″ by 39¼″

The Next Giant

In 1975, Lawrence Bender & Associates were retained to design an annual report for Advanced Micro Devices, a West Coast company which makes integrated circuits—those bits of electronic wizardry that power anything. The client wanted a unifying element for the report, some symbol which could crystallize the company's aggressive self-image as a fairly recent arrival on the scene who would soon be the leader in the integrated circuit industry.

After getting into the project, designers Larry Bender and Mark Wallin soon discovered that Advanced Micro Devices, for all their bravado, didn't have a clear-cut picture of what they wanted. Bender and Wallin, however, did.

Basing their concept partly on the client's vision of growing bigger each year and also on the design plan for the developmental stages of a circuit, they evolved a 10-color symbol, each color standing for one of the client's product areas. Bender and Wallin then found that in order to explain why their solution worked, they had to comp up a number of the client's own unworkable suggestions, so "the next giant" (as Advanced Micro Devices likes to be known) could see the difference.

The client's approval resulted in a two-year continuing campaign utilizing the circuit symbol. In 1976, Bender and Wallin picked it up for the poster shown. Their only pre-design instructions were to incorporate the two lines of copy. Five hundred fifty posters were silkscreened; 150 signed and numbered prints (these minus copy) were also prepared. The symbol will also be seen on quarterly reports, literature, and even on people in the form of T-shirts.—*VFB*

Advanced Micro Devices   The Next Giant

Posters/78

Client: Advanced Micro Devices
Design firm: Lawrence Bender & Associates, Palo Alto, CA
Art director: Larry Bender
Designers: Larry Bender, Mark Wallin
Illustrator: Mark Wallin
Copywriter: J. Sanders
Colors: Ten flat colors
Size: 24" by 40"

Transylvania University

Bananas is a humor magazine published by Scholastic Book Services for seventh-, eighth-, and ninth-graders. Available through Scholastic's junior high school book club by subscription or single issue, it is designed to appeal to students who aren't particularly interested in reading. Assuming that these youngsters are products of the television generation whose interest in the printed word may be kindled with stories about films and TV shows they see regularly, the editors plan issues to include lots of exciting photography and articles relating to the media. As an added inducement, each copy of the magazine features a poster illustrating some aspect of the editorial content, which can be pulled out of the centerfold for kids to hang on their walls.

To tie in with a story about the actors who have portrayed Frankenstein's monster in the movies, Bananas' art director, Bob Feldgus, asked illustrator Richard Sparks to produce a poster which would be bizarre and humorous at the same time. Sparks, whose work had appeared in the magazine on previous occasions, painted the monster—sporting a grotesque collection of scars and metallic sutures—blow-drying his hair in the narrow confines of a cell. Although Feldgus calls Bananas "an art director's magazine" which allows him a great deal of freedom, he was called upon in this case to request a revision in Sparks' original illustration. Because of the youth of its audience and the educational channels through which the publication is distributed, Sparks was asked to dress his bare-chested monster in an undershirt. The addition of clothing resulted in an unexpected visual joke. The shirt, adorned with varsity letters, seemed to unite the actors in an oddly unconventional alumni association.

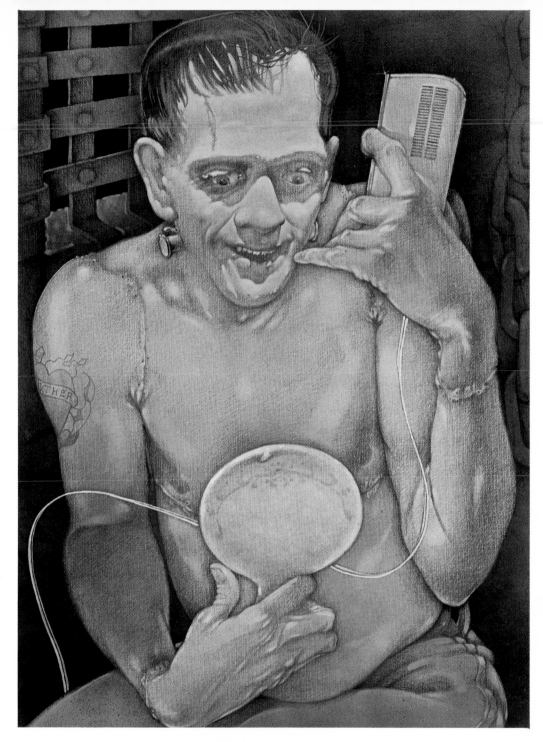

Client: Bananas Magazine, Scholastic Book Services
Art director/designer: Bob Feldgus
Illustrator: Richard Sparks
Copywriter: Bob Stine
Printer: Arcata Graphics
Colors: Full color
Size: 15½" by 21½"

Above: original illustration without T-shirt. Left: final poster.

Saint Heironymous Press

Pandora's Box

David Lance Goines has been in the printing business for 13 years. Five years ago, when the company he was working for went out of business, Goines bought the plant and equipment and became thenceforward master of his own establishment, the Saint Heironymous Press.

A small, carefully run, one-man operation, the press itself is an essential factor in Goines's designs, affecting both the practical and inventive aspects of his work. On a strictly pragmatic level, his production is limited by his own capacity to carry out every operation involved in offset printing. "I do all the work for every poster," Goines explains with obvious satisfaction, "beginning with the original art, on through the camera work, stripping, color separations, mixing of inks, platemaking, printing and trimming. I even make the final delivery in my Volkswagen." From a creative point of view, however, Goines's thorough involvement in his own operation allows him enormous freedom—to design what he wants, more or less when he wants, and to control the very special quality of the final printing.

Goines, much of whose work reflects the meticulous, graceful stylization of Art Nouveau/Art Deco motifs, often makes up for time lost on a job that doesn't work out by reviving the same basic idea for another assignment. "There's no sense in wasting a perfectly good design," he observes. "Using it somewhere else is really *pro bono*

publico." The image for *Pandora's Box,* a 1928 German film, was originally done for a greeting card company but rejected. Goines, who has a standing commission from the Pacific Film Archive to produce movie posters whenever he chooses to do so, found that the heavy brooding skyline and withered flower worked much better as a symbol for G.W. Pabst's strange and frightening movie. The clumsy, distorted cityscape suggested the intense, warped perspectives of German expressionism and the bizarre drooping flower made an appropriate symbol for Pandora, a woman with a predilection for destruction who is, in the end, herself destroyed.

Usually, posters for the Pacific Film Archive, a rather specialized operation funded both by the state government and private foundations, are displayed only on site—at its small 200-seat theater. Goines's poster for "Music and the Movies," however, received broader publicity. Designed to promote a two-month series of film showings, it was exhibited also by the series' co-sponsors, City magazine, and KSAN, a San Francisco radio station. Goines's illustration had originally been done for a classical guitarist who decided to use a photograph instead. Its transformation into a film poster was accomplished with only a change in copy. Although the event is long since past, Goines reports that the poster is still in demand, especially, for some reason, by teenage boys.

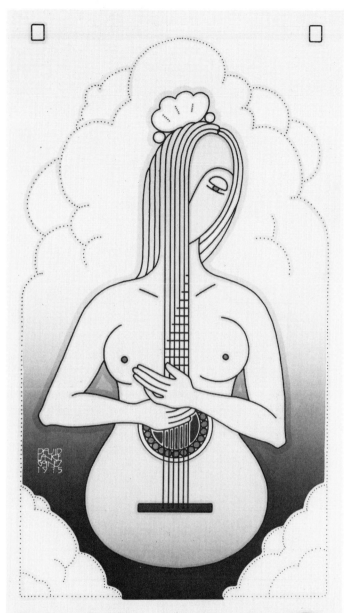

Opposite page:
Client: Pacific Film Archive
Design firm: Saint Heironymous Press, Berkeley, CA
Art director/designer/printer: David Lance Goines
Colors: Gray, split-fountain blues, light, medium and dark creme, orange, dull black
Size: 13" by 24"

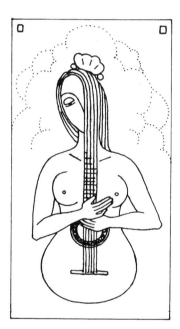

Client: Pacific Film Archive
Design firm: Saint Heironymous Press, Berkeley, CA
Art director/designer/printer: David Lance Goines
Colors: Blue split-fountain, blue, brown split-fountain, brown, creme, gray, black
Size: 10" by 24"

Yet another waste not-want not illustration appears on Goines's poster for his favorite restaurant, "Chez:Panisse." Originally commissioned by a picture framer who went out of business before the design was printed, the vase of roses was resurrected a year later when Goines realized that it would be an appropriate symbol for a bistro which takes pride in decorating every table with freshly cut flowers. Designed to advertise the restaurant's fourth birthday, the poster featured a mouth-watering menu of gourmet delicacies.

Goines enjoys gourmet delicacies and his special feeling for champagne resulted in a success worth celebrating. Deciding on his own initiative to print a poster advertising Champagne Deutz, Goines chose for his illustration figures connected with a carefree time of life. A corked bottle on its side doubles as a cannon, the decidedly unmenacing property of two efficient little wooden soldiers. "Champagne is associated with cheerful

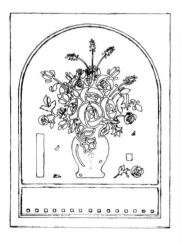

Client: Chez:Panisse Restaurant
Design firm: Saint Heironymous Press, Berkeley, CA
Art director/designer/printer: David Lance Goines
Copywriters: Alice Louise Waters, Jeremiah Tower
Colors: Gray, dark gray, creme, yellow, light rose, dark rose, light salmon, dark salmon
Size: 18″ by 24″ (determined by size of press)

occasions and happy memories,'' he explains, ''hence the symbols of childhood.'' The toy cannon, of course, suggests the unfrightening pop of a cork. Goines originally printed only 300 copies of the poster. which was displayed at Chez:Panisse, in the homes of friends, and by one or two galleries. Eventually, the San Francisco distributor, Connoisseur Wine Imports, saw Goines's poster and showed it to the proprietor of Deutz in France. ''Just recently he ordered 500 copies,'' Goines reports, ''but it meant four solid days of press work.'' With seven flat colors to print and fairly heavy coverage, Goines had to allow each color to dry before going on to the next run through the press.

Such painstaking supervision was obviously impossible during the printing of Goines's album cover for Cannonball Adderley's *Big Man*. A recording of a folk musical based on the legend of John Henry, the album was produced by Fantasy Records in quantities much larger than

Client/art director/designer/ printer: David Lance Goines
Design firm: Saint Heironymous Press, Berkeley, CA
Colors: Gray, light green, dark green, gold, ocher, red, dark gray, flat black
Size: 18″ by 24″

Big Man

the Heironymous Press can handle. The recording had not yet been made when Goines was asked to design the cover, and unable to draw inspiration from the music or the performance, he took the symbols for his illustration from the legend itself. The story grew up among miners drilling the Big Bend Tunnel of the Chesapeake & Ohio Railway in West Virginia sometime around 1870. It involves an American black man who pits himself with hammer and steel bit against a steam drill. Though in the end he beats the machine, the effort costs him his life. Goines's illustration depicts not only the brown hands, white steam cloud, spike, hammer and broken heart of the legend but also the authentic Chesapeake & Ohio logo of the period. That particular detail was requested by Cannonball Adderley who died before the album was finished. Dissatisfied with Fantasy's printing, Goines subsequently printed his own edition of 213 posters using the same artwork.

Client: Fantasy Records
Design firm: Saint Heironymous Press, Berkeley, CA
Art director: Phil Carroll
Designer: David Lance Goines

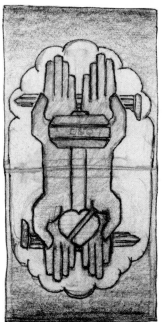

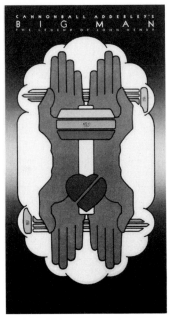

Above: album cover printed by Fantasy records. Far left: sketch. Left: poster which Goines printed himself at St. Heironymous Press because he was dissatisfied with Fantasy's reproduction of his art.

In 1974, Norman Sanders began photographing people in their favorite rooms at home. His instructions to his subjects, most of whom he had not known previously, were simply: ''Do what is comfortable and natural for you in this setting, and avoid tidying up the room especially for the photograph.'' The resulting pictures, a series of 100 black-and-white photos made over a period of two years, were exhibited in May 1976, at the Travelling Intermedia Gallery, a branch of Rockland Community College in Suffern, New York.

To advertise the exhibit in community centers, galleries, schools, and store windows throughout Rockland County, Sanders asked Hoi Ling Chu to design a poster which would suggest the special intimacy of the photographs without forfeiting its ability to attract attention. Chu's decision to shape the poster like a house solved both aspects of the problem at once. The announcement's unusual silhouette not only made it conspicuous amid the clutter of institutional bulletin boards but also served to indicate the nature of the exhibition which was called ''At Home.'' ''I found it intriguing,'' Chu observes, ''that by trimming the paper a little differently, I was able to make a graphic statement about the photographs.''

Because Sanders' own firm was to do the final printing, Chu and Sanders, who worked together on the entire project, decided to leave the budget for that aspect of the operation open. They agreed that the design should be limited to two colors and should not involve anything that a normally equipped litho plant was unable to handle. Because Chu felt that enlargement or reduction would affect the quality of the photograph, the size of the poster was determined by the size of Sanders' original print.

Though originally intended only for public display, the poster, which was printed in an edition of 250, was subsequently sold retail and has become something of a collector's item.

At Home
Photographs by Norman Sanders

May 19 to June 2, 1976
Monday through Thursday, 9 AM to 9 PM; Friday, 9 AM to 5 PM; Saturday, 11 AM to 2 PM
Presented by The Travelling Intermedia Gallery
at the Library Media Center
Rockland Community College, Suffern, New York
This exhibition is funded in part by the New York State Council on the Arts.

Client/photographer: Norman Sanders
Art director/designer: Hoi Ling Chu
Printer: Sanders Printing Corp.
Colors: Two blacks
Size: 18½" by 23¼" at apex

Winged Fish

The Abitibi Paper Company's "sail series" is a direct-mail program based on sailing lore and offering specifications and technical information on a variety of different grades of stock. Making the most of a comprehensive topic which includes everything from oceanography and zoological facts to definitions of boating terms, the program consists of eight sequential mailings each of which demonstrates the properties of one of Abitibi's products. Developed by art director Robert Burns, the entire kit includes eight dividers and a portfolio box for filing the series' assorted components.

The first mailing piece, entitled "Wind and Wave," opens like a 9″ by 12″ booklet and unfolds again to disclose metallic fish and a sky full of seagulls, demonstrating the effect of silver ink printed over solid blue on Royal Offset Enamel. Opened to its full extent, the folder becomes a four-color poster depicting a winged fish skimming the surface of a tranquil sea. Heather Cooper's imaginative painting makes an excellent visual description of the parallels between sail and wing, keel and fin. Her precise style and the wide range of subtle colors resulted in a technically challenging reproduction which effectively demonstrates the paper's printability.

Although the mailing was sent to production managers in advertising agencies, publishing companies and industry, there was considerable demand for extra copies that could be framed uncreased. A total of 12,000 posters was printed.

Client: Abitibi Provincial Paper, Advertising Department
Design firm: Burns & Cooper Ltd., Toronto
Art director/designer: Robert Burns
Illustrator: Heather Cooper
Printer: Plow & Watters Ltd.
Colors: Full color
Size: 24″ by 36″

Mailing piece components.

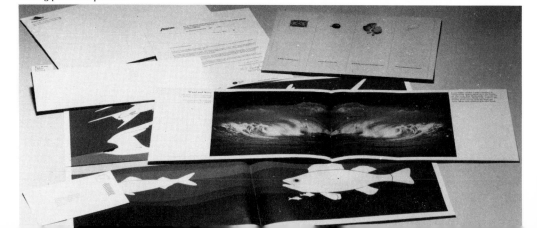

Dear Thomas Jefferson

Container Corporation of America has, over the years, consistently maintained the policy that industry has a responsibility to the society in which it takes root and flourishes. A cornerstone of Container's business philosophy, this concept is one which the company's management hopes its many employees will also come to understand.

Early in 1976, CCA's employee communications department decided to sponsor a contest which would not only involve employees in a kind of intellectual celebration of the Bicentennial but would also encourage them to think about the role of industry in society. The rules were simply to write in 250 words or less a statement to convince Thomas Jefferson, a proponent of an agrarian way of life, that industry is good for America's growth. First prize was an all-expense-paid trip for two to one of the Bicentennial cities; second prize was $100; and third prize was a $50 U.S. savings bond.

To draw employees' attention to the contest in an unusually beguiling fashion, corporate art director Bill Bonnell planned a series of four teaser posters to be put up, one panel per week, over a 28-day period. The first panel announced the contest and revealed the prizes. The second panel explained the rules and the third panel listed the judges. To the fourth panel, which repeated the contest instructions, was attached a sheaf of numbered entry blanks. The whole series, which was printed in red, white, and blue on white foam core, was unified by a blow-up of the salutation, "Dear Thomas Jefferson," embellished with an intricate network of graceful 18th-century swashes. Each panel worked graphically as a single poster, but for anyone except the most serious student of 18th-century calligraphy it was impossible to decipher the handwriting until at least three panels were in place. Two sets of posters were put up in each of the over 100 Container plants, to be viewed by a total of approximately 17,000 employees. The restrained Swiss typography contrasts nicely with the flamboyant penmanship and intriguing physical layout of the posters which succeeded in drawing a gratifying number of entries.

Client: Employee Communications Department, Container Corporation of America
Design firm: Corporate Design Department, CCA, Chicago
Art director/designer: Bill Bonnell III
Copywriter: Susan Black
Colors: Red, white, blue on white foam core
Size: 3' by 5'

America: the third century

"America: the third century"—a collection of posters by 13 distinguished American artists, including Robert Rauschenberg, James Rosenquist and Roy Lichtenstein—is part of a major Bicentennial art program sponsored by the Mobil Oil Corporation, a company whose patronage of the arts has become increasingly apparent in recent years. To commemorate the Bicentennial celebration and herald the third century of American national life, Mobil, working closely with art director Steven Fineberg at Chermayeff & Geismar Associates, asked each artist to create an image interpreting his impression of an American theme. Produced in several workshops throughout the U.S. under the supervision of the artists, these prints were first issued as a limited, signed and numbered 200-edition portfolio. In order to circulate the series among a wider audience, the prints were subsequently reproduced as posters designed by Fineberg to include the headline and the official Bicentennial administration logo. The layout was planned to allow the type to be cut off. Explains Fineberg, "These then become nice prints that can be owned at a very fair and reasonable cost."

The entire project took almost two years, a time-span which included the initial selection of the artists, the negotiation of contracts, the production of the images and the final printing. The size

"The Home My Daddy Built," by Velox Ward.

was restricted to the standard measurements of poster and print flat files used by museum shops and poster dealers, and the artists were asked to relate their designs to the project theme. Otherwise, there were no limitations and the resulting works of art represent an exciting variety of techniques, media and individual creative expression.

The four posters selected by the judges for inclusion in this Casebook typify the series' diversity of style and subject matter. These interpretations of the Bicentennial motif are highly personal and often relate to the project's general concept only in an oblique manner. Velox Ward's painting, "The Home My Daddy Built," is the most obviously expressive of an American theme. A primitive treatment of a stark, clapboard homestead typical of rural American architecture, it suggests both the loneliness and somewhat idealized simplicity of our early farming communities. "Still Life with Eggs, Candlestick and Bowl" by William Bailey, a nostalgic painting of outmoded cooking utensils in muted shades of brown, cream and violet, is also reminiscent of an old-fashioned way of life. "Duck out of Water," a lithograph with silkscreen and collage by Raymond Saunders, the only black artist in the group, depicts a colored duck, its red, blue, yellow and green stripes made vibrant and obtrusive by the uniformity of the gray background. One of the most

America: the third century

"Still Life with Eggs, Candlestick and Bowl," by William Bailey.

interesting images in the series is Christo's "Texas Mastaba," a lithograph featuring a projected design for 500,000 stacked oil drums. This sketch is typical of Christo's art which includes both two-dimensional conceptual images and complex three-dimensional monumental sculptures expressive of his deep concern with the social and ecological effects of industrial technology. As in this illustration of oil drums, Christo sketches plans for a massive ecologically-oriented structure, sells the drawings, and with the proceeds builds the monument, a fitting tribute to the society which made it possible—and, in this case, an interesting concept for an original print commissioned by an oil company.

The proceeds from the sale of the original portfolios have been donated to charities selected by the 13 artists, with a substantial portion going to Change, Inc., a non-profit organization founded by Robert Rauschenberg to provide emergency funds for artists in need of assistance. The posters, distributed by Pace Gallery, are sold at cost.

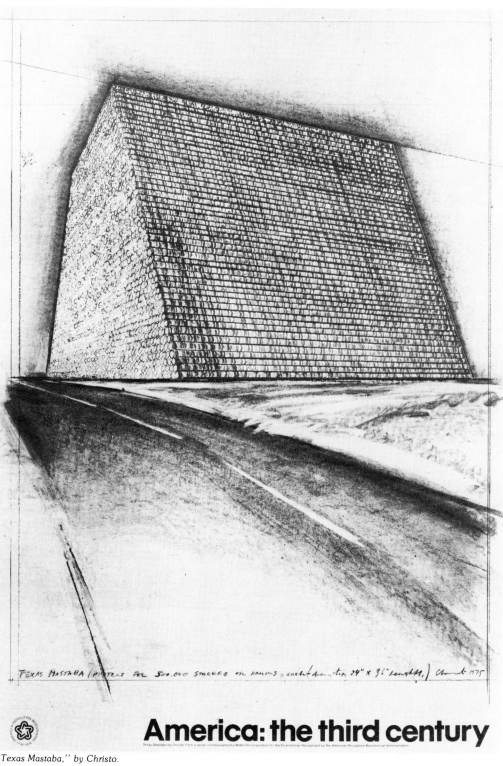

"Texas Mastaba," by Christo.

"Yankee Flame," by Ben Schonzeit.

America: the third century
"Sunrise," by Robert Andrew Parker.

America: the third century
"City," by Constantino Nivola.

America: the third century

"Duck out of Water," by Raymond Saunders.

America: the third century
"America Whistles," by Edward Ruscha.

Client: Mobil Oil Corp.
Design firm/publisher: APC Editions, Chermayeff & Geismar Associates, New York
Art director/designer: Steven Fineberg
Artists: William Bailey, Christo, Raymond Saunders, Velox Ward
Printer: Sanders Printing Co.
Colors: Full color
Size: 24" by 35"

A picture of a man stuck upside-down with his hands chained together in what seems at first glance to be a blue telephone booth full of water can't fail to attract attention. If the man happens to be super-magician Doug Henning and the illustrator is Seymour Chwast, the combination is bound to be a success. Gordon Bowman, manager of creative programs for Mobil Oil Corporation, probably suspected as much when he asked Chwast to design a poster advertising a Mobil television showcase featuring a live performance by Henning. Although the magician's program was based on a certain amount of conjury and cunning derived from his Broadway production, *The Magic Show*, it also included Houdini's sensational water-torture escape, an act which Bowman described to Chwast in some detail. Armed with this description and some photographs of Henning, Chwast set about producing a poster which would reflect the drama and charm of the performance.

His solution, which parodies to some extent the old posters advertising Houdini himself, was quite the reverse of magic. Deceptively simple in appearance, it was exceptionally difficult to produce. Chwast did the pen-and-ink illustration in a flat, naive style and thoroughly planned the typography—a variety of faces and sizes reflecting the ornamental character of hand-set wooden letters on early broadsides. "He was extraordinary in working out the two side panels," recalls designer Pam Vassil who worked with Chwast on the project and hand-lettered the word "Houdini." "He has an incredible sense of weight and balance. It's pure instinct. He really knows what typefaces go well together."

The type and drawing, done one-half size and blown up to poster dimensions later

on, were only the beginning of a long and complicated production process. Several people completed the final mechanical, which involved an intricately worked out series of amberlith overlays. A separate set of overlays for percentages of gray had to be cut for a different version of the poster to run as a newspaper ad. Although Chwast had originally intended to print the poster in

12 flat colors, he later decided to use a combination of PMS inks and process colors. After one initial proofing, several color adjustments were made on press. "Mobil cooperated fully in letting us do this," Chwast reports, "and reaction to the poster was very favorable."

THE SENSATIONAL HOUDINI
WATER TORTURE ESCAPE

ATTEMPTED
FOR THE FIRST TIME
"LIVE"
ON TELEVISION!!!
DURING THE
Mobil SHOWCASE
Presentation Of
"THE WORLD OF MAGIC"
DECEMBER 26
ON NBC AT 8PM EST.
SPECIAL GUEST STARS
ORSON WELLES
BILL COSBY
JULIE NEWMAR

BY
DOUG HENNING
STARRING IN
"THE MAGIC SHOW"
ONE OF BROADWAY'S BRIGHTEST RECENT HITS

Remember: This will be a "live" broadcast of a breathtaking feat never attempted before under these circumstances.

Client: Mobil Oil Corp.
Design firm: Push Pin Studios, New York
Art director: Gordon Bowman
Illustrator/designer: Seymour Chwast
Letterer: Pamela Vassil
Copywriter: Suzie Burlie
Printer: Crafton Graphic Co.
Colors: Four-color process and matched colors
Size: 24″ by 36″

Few entertainers are content to sit back and enjoy the echo of previously won applause. Anticipating the excitement of a new performance and a potentially wider audience, they are constantly on the lookout for challenging original productions. Magician Doug Henning is no exception. Having achieved perfection, as well as fame and fortune, with a brilliantly enacted panorama of Houdini tricks, he decided to put together a new magic show. Immersing himself in research, and delving into ancient oriental lore—long-lost magic rediscovered—he worked out a breathtaking exhibition of conjury and enchantment that was essentially his own. Scheduled to introduce his new show during a tour of 50 colleges in the spring of 1976, Henning approached art director Jack Rennert at Darien House and asked him to do a poster announcing the performance. Having prepared his own headline, a phrase which indicates both the nature of his act and its effect on the audience, Henning suggested that the poster not concentrate on a single trick but stress the duality between illusion and reality. "If there was one word he kept repeating over and over again, it was 'wonder,'" Rennert recalls. "He wanted to give a sense of wonder to the spectators at his show and to viewers of the poster." They decided also that the art should include a recognizable figure of Henning.

With only 18 days in which to finish the entire job, printing included, Rennert called upon a local artist, Gary Cooley, to do the illustration. At Rennert's request, Cooley met the magician to discuss his ideas firsthand. "It was a pretty nice arrangement," Cooley says. "He explained his new magic and I took pieces of it and put together an image. He wanted the feeling of awe to be strong." Some of

Henning's new material involved working with bubbles; the flower alludes to his adaptation of old Chinese magic in which lotus blossoms were often the final stage in a complicated series of metamorphoses.

The poster, which was printed as a "subway one-sheet" to cover the possibility of its being used later to publicize a New York appearance, had to be

proofed on press to save time. Four colors did not succeed in faithfully reproducing the original, so a second blue was run the following day with excellent results. The announcement worked well as a drawing card during Henning's tour, and the over-run has made a profitable addition to the Darien House series of "Contemporary Poster Classics."

Client: Doug Henning
Design firm: Darien House, Inc., New York
Art director: Jack Rennert
Designer/illustrator: Gary Cooley
Printer: MacNaughton Lithograph Co.
Color: Four-color process with an extra blue
Size: 30" by 45"

N.Y. Architectural Contrasts

This poster was ingeniously developed in tandem with a fold-out mailing piece. What makes both items a still greater accomplishment of the designer, though, is that they were born largely *because* of rather than despite a limited budget.

George Tscherny's original assignment from Monadnock Paper Mills was a promotional brochure needed as a demonstration of the range of printing contrasts made possible with their Astrolite paper. Tscherny's selection of a theme for this dramatization was architecture, a subject of personal interest and one which he felt would be of general interest as well. (It is worth noting that, as Tscherny points out, since a paper manufacturer's greatest concern lies with demonstrating printability, the choice of subject matter is usually left up to the designer.) His selection of New York City, though, was only partly due to the fascination its buildings hold for him; the budget would never sustain travel to additional locales.

Tscherny in turn felt that the client's idea of a brochure was too expensive; costs could be kept down by doing a folded piece. Monadnock also welcomed Tscherny's further suggestion of using easily obtainable art for the inside of the mailer. Aside from Tscherny's own photography, previously taken shots from other sources could also be used.

But perhaps Tscherny's best idea was that of utilizing the same photograph for both

Architectural Contrasts
on Monadnock's White, Bright, <u>Astrolite</u>

poster and mailer: two promotional pieces could be developed comfortably within the budget that at the outset had been proposed for one brochure.

When it was time to select the scene for the poster/mailer shot, finding the right pictorial elements proved relatively easy. The year before, Tscherny had done a four-color shot of what he calls "the ultimate in contrast to be found in New York," a church two blocks below the World Trade Center complex. By reshooting from a slightly different angle he was able to obtain the composition he wanted. Actually, it was at this point that a complex technical problem arose. In designing the poster, Tscherny had found its size could only be determined by the mailer's folding dimensions. "Furthermore, it was important to compose the photography in such a way that the folded sections worked independently, as well as with the whole photograph," Tscherny explains.

Photography was done in black-and-white, four-color being yet another strain on the budget. Here again, the designer was able to make a limitation work in his favor. He saw that the very deep black, medium gray and light tones enhanced the client's objective, by proving that Astrolite was, as he puts it, "a perfect printing sheet for black-and-white."

After the client's final approval, 1000 posters were sent to art directors and 19,000 mailing pieces went to

paper specifiers and buyers.

Clearly, throughout all phases of his assignment, Tscherny's solutions demonstrate strongly how to turn seeming hindrances in a budget to excellent advantage.—VFB

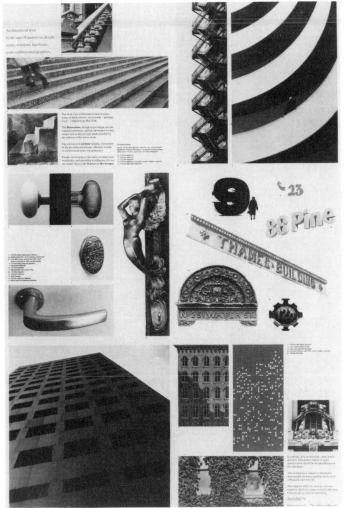

Client: Monadnock Paper Mills, Inc.
Design firm: George Tscherny, Inc., New York
Designer/art director/copywriter/photographer: George Tscherny
Printer: Sanders Printing Corp.
Colors: Black-and-white
Size: 20″ by 30″

Opposite page: poster. Left above: back of poster. Left: mailer.

The Corkscrew/
The Eggbeater

Arrow Development
Company is, like most large
corporations, relatively
conservative. The products it
manufactures, though, are
designed to be as outlandish
as possible—they're million-
dollar mind-and-body-
bending giant amusement park
rides. One called the
Corkscrew is literally that; this
vision that would have pleased
a torturer of the Middle Ages
twists and flips its victims
forward, then backward—from
a height of 70 feet.

Lawrence Bender &
Associates had done some
ads for Arrow but one day
were simply "blue skying," as
designer Mark Wallin
appropriately puts it, when
they hit on the idea of doing
a promotional poster
campaign based on takeoffs
of their client's rides. The
series could be sent to
Arrow's salesmen, prospects
and customers to reaffirm the
company's industry
leadership. Smaller parks,
normally not able to afford
the rides, would also receive
the posters if only to spur
awareness of the name.

Bender and Wallin then
worked up a series of
thumbnail sketches, which
they submitted, and found
their client surprisingly
responsive. Once the
Corkscrew was set to start off
the series, the team wanted to
follow up with the Loop (a
still more bizarre ride
currently being tested but not
installed anywhere). They
wanted to depict a nutcracker
for the Loop, but the client
somehow saw it as more of
an eggbeater. Finally, a crank
beater won out over a

Another great ride
from Arrow Development Company
ARROW

preliminary design of a wire whisk, because of its more mechanical feeling.

The four-color illustrations by Los Angeles illustrator John Mattos were done in airbrush, felt to be more graphically exciting by the designers. The results are more than a little reminiscent of photorealism but are ultimately more pleasing since the hand tool, the major visual element in each poster, better than lifelike is larger than life, like the rides themselves, and slips over the edge from reality to fantasy.

Bender and Wallin don't plan on bringing their series to a close after the Loop, however. Mark Wallin sees at least one or two more posters coming up for rides now in development. In fact, the next poster he and Larry Bender will probably produce is called the Can Opener. Let your imagination take it from there.—*VFB*

Client: Arrow Development Co.
Design firm: Lawrence Bender & Associates, Palo Alto, CA
Agency: Moser & Associates
Art directors/designers/copywriters: Larry Bender, Mark Wallin
Illustrator: John Mattos
Printer: Ceres Litho
Colors: Full color
Size: 20″ by 30″

If you liked our Corkscrew™
get a load of what we're whipping up for you now

ARROW

When Joseph Bottoni was asked to design a poster informing colleges and art schools throughout the country about a Master of Fine Arts program in ceramics at the University of Cincinnati, he decided to let potential students know that Cincinnati is a nice place in which to live and work. Operating with a four-week deadline and a very tight budget ($300), he quite appropriately enlisted the help of students in the ceramics department and asked them to make figurines of objects which might be found in any real or imagined landscape. The resulting miniatures, a charming and imaginative collection of animals, trees and architectural whimsy, were created in record time. Because type and photo costs had to be kept to a minimum, Bottoni had each figurine shot separately and worked out the final panorama in his studio, shifting the elements around until he hit on just the right pattern.

So that it could be used as both poster and mailer, the printed art was produced not only in flat sheets but also scored and folded to an 8½" by 11" size. The tiny rainbow bleeding off the right edge was hand-tinted on all 500 copies. Presumably, its missing end hovers over Cincinnati, pointing the way to fame and fortune.

Client: Ceramics Department, College of Design, Architecture, and Art, University of Cincinnati
Art director/designer: Joseph Bottoni
Photographer: Harriet Saks
Colors: Black-and-white; rainbow hand tinted in five pastels
Size: 34" by 11" flat; 8½" by 11" folded

Hunt's Tomato

Hunt's

When a series of Hunt-Wesson print ads featuring recipes using tomato sauce appeared in national women's magazines a couple of years ago, they elicited a gratifying number of fan letters from readers and food editors, who reported that the recipes were being enthusiastically clipped and filed away. There was so much interest in the ads that art director William McCaffery, who had worked on the campaign, decided that there might be an even better way to promote the product and please the consumer. "The ads were full of information," McCaffery explains. "It was my idea to produce a series of kitchen posters which would make that information more readily available to people and in an attractive way." He presented his idea to Hunt-Wesson, and with their wholehearted approval proceeded to design the posters.

Since McCaffery's plan was to "get the poster into the consumer's environment" where it could be inspected at length from close quarters, both illustrations and copy, unlike the images on most posters, are small and detailed. Each poster offers a kind of monograph on one specific food compatible with Hunt's tomato sauce. The pasta poster identifies, with label and photographs, over 40 kinds of macaroni and spaghetti and supplies, as well, information about their history, preparation and nutritional value. Another in the series presents an assortment of herbs. The poster selected by the judges for inclusion here is the simplest of the three. It features a photograph of a large tomato surrounded by a halo of carefully researched copy revealing the chronological history of man's involvement with the "love apple," and a collection of recipes.

Offered for sale in print ads and distributed in schools through home economics programs, the poster has been so successful that the supply ran out before all requests could be filled. McCaffery himself is pleased with the advertising concept. "The posters are useful *and* decorative," he remarks, "and they keep the client's name and product in front of the consumer all the time."

Pasta poster.

Client: Hunt-Wesson Foods
Art director/designer: William McCaffery
Photographer: Irwin Horowitz
Copywriter: Kelly Welles
Printer: Graphic Arts
Colors: Full color
Size: 24" by 36"

Citicorp Center
Arts & Crafts/Crown

Using a construction site as a potential environment for graphic design is a concept that has been considered only recently, and on rare occasions. Fortunately, when Citicorp Center—an almost square block of plazas, offices, shops and a church in midtown Manhattan—was planned, it was clear that a stronger approach was needed than "Post no bills."

The firm of Anspach Grossman Portugal, which had previously developed corporate identity systems for both Citicorp and Citibank, would again utilize corporate imagery for Citicorp Center's construction area—but on a more dramatic and popularized scale. A series of eight posters, mounted on barricades running along the site's perimeter, would trace Citicorp Center's development from a hole in the ground to its varied roles after completion. For instance, "Crown," one of the posters in the series, details the energy conservation system planned for the office tower; the crown itself is a possible future converter of solar energy. In a lighter vein, another poster, "Arts & Crafts," features examples of some of the cultural events that will take place at Citicorp Center.

Aside from restoring some of the visual appeal usually lost at the beginning of construction, it was hoped that the annoyance factor of traversing those labyrinthine construction passages would be played down by the posters' graphics and highly

informational copy.

While the client gave overall approval to design director Eugene J. Grossman's recommendation, a tight rein was kept over the budget, as it was to include architectural renderings as well as photography. As a result, three-color was used whenever possible. The posters were all made a substantial 3' by 4', though, to both stand out from the construction and be easily recognized from streets opposite the site. All the posters utilized the same striped pattern along the upper and/or lower border and the angled words Citicorp Center in order to create a unifying motif.

Having made their on-site appearance in the fall of 1976, the posters will remain there until the complex's completion sometime in 1978.—VFB

Opposite page, bottom: construction site. Above: spectator viewing poster exhibit.

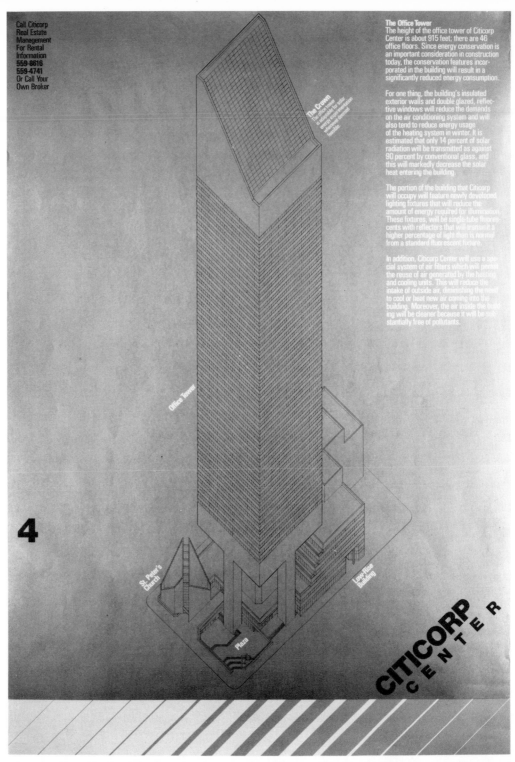

Call Citicorp
Real Estate
Management
For Rental
Information
559-8616
559-4741
Or Call Your
Own Broker

The Office Tower
The height of the office tower of Citicorp Center is about 915 feet; there are 46 office floors. Since energy conservation is an important consideration in construction today, the conservation features incorporated in the building will result in a significantly reduced energy consumption.

For one thing, the building's insulated exterior walls and double glazed, reflective windows will reduce the demands on the air conditioning system and will also tend to reduce energy usage of the heating system in winter. It is estimated that only 14 percent of solar radiation will be transmitted as against 90 percent by conventional glass, and this will markedly decrease the solar heat entering the building.

The portion of the building that Citicorp will occupy will feature newly developed lighting fixtures that will reduce the amount of energy required for illumination. These fixtures will be single-tube fluorescents with reflectors that will transmit a higher percentage of light than is normal from a standard fluorescent fixture.

In addition, Citicorp Center will use a special system of air filters which will permit the reuse of air generated by the heating and cooling units. This will reduce the intake of outside air, diminishing the need to cool or heat new air coming into the building. Moreover, the air inside the building will be cleaner because it will be substantially free of pollutants.

The Crown

Office Tower

St. Peter's Church

Plaza

Low-Rise Building

CITICORP CENTER

Client: Citicorp
Design firm: Anspach Grossman Portugal, Inc., New York
Design director: Eugene J. Grossman
Designer: Daniel Friedman
Photographer: Lawrence Bach
Illustrator: Henry Dong
Copywriter: Michael Remba—Citibank
Printer: Crafton Graphic Co., Inc.
Colors: Black, gray and red
Size: 32″ by 48″

Ken Whitmore

When photographer Ken Whitmore decided to produce a poster for use as a promotion piece, he chose as an example of his work an odd and provocative illustration. Neither a straight photograph nor a genuine montage, Whitmore's shot frames a deserted stretch of beach, the loneliness of which is emphasized by two shells and an abandoned doll. But the sand is too coarse; the shells are too big; the sky and water are too blue. Like images from a dream, the photograph is disturbing, its symbols familiar but surreal and unsettling. Whitmore had originally shot the beach as background for a fashion job. Enlarged and hand-tinted, it made an excellent setting for three perfectly ordinary but out-of-scale props. The final photograph was shot in color in Whitmore's studio.

To carry out the poster's photographic theme, the edge was designed to look like a filmstrip. The letters and digits of Whitmore's name and phone number were projected and painstakingly lifted character by character from numbers and letters on an Eastman negative. Two hundred fifty copies of the poster were printed and mailed to art directors and prospective clients with very good response.

Client: Ken Whitmore Photography
Art director/designer: Mel Whitmore
Photographer: Ken Whitmore
Colors: Full color
Size: 18" by 21"

Don't Make a Mockery of America

Several months ago, Karen Bunde and Andrea Giambrone, co-workers in a Los Angeles advertising agency, decided that the celebration of America's 200th birthday was, in many cases, not being carried out with the dignity and good taste appropriate to the occasion. Like modern Christmases which are unflaggingly promoted from the day after Thanksgiving until January 2, the Bicentennial seemed to them unscrupulously presumed upon. Everyone had jumped on the patriotic bandwagon and the resulting commercialism was clearly out of hand.

Not content to sit back and complain, they took upon themselves the task of designing a poster which would remind advertising agencies, manufacturers, and people in the communications industries to exercise judgment and restraint in producing goods and information connected with the Bicentennial. To emphasize the importance of their message and to help cover production costs, Bunde and Giambrone created, for the sole purpose of this project, a small organization virtuously, but appropriately, named Advertising People Who Care. "They were a group of creative contributors and suppliers," Bunde explains, "who gave generously of their considerable talents out of pure conviction. No one was paid. All the work was voluntary because everyone believed in the value of the project."

Persuaded that the best ploy was to fight fire with fire, the designers chose a toilet seat adorned with red, white, blue and gold patriotic images to symbolize Bicentennial abuse. "Our audience was made up of professional communicators," Bunde notes; "we had to speak their language in the boldest way possible." Illustrator Charley Brown decorated the toilet seat, a painstaking task which led him to proclaim that he would never again paint a curved surface. But the real chore for a group of such limited size was stuffing and mailing 600 poster tubes.

Judging from mail and phone calls, Bunde reports that response to the poster has been overwhelmingly positive. "Given all the time and money in the world, we would have done it exactly the same way," she says; "we made absolutely no compromises."

Please, don't make a mockery of America.

Client: Advertising People Who Care
Art Director/designer: Karen Bunde
Copywriter: Andrea Giambrone
Illustrator: Charley Brown
Photographer: Phil Shuper
Color: Full color
Size: 22″ by 28″

On a Sunday in November, 1975, Paramount Pictures ran a full-page ad in the New York Times announcing its hottest new "motion picture event," a remake of *King Kong,* not scheduled for release until a full year after the ad appeared. The ad, which included an address for postcards requesting color reprints, drew a response from 25,000 Times readers all over the country. That kind of return—indicating an alert, national readership—provides a priceless resource for the newspaper in soliciting future advertising. Long before this particular triumph, similar responses gave rise to a Times policy of following up successful ads with promotional campaigns publicizing the value of the paper as an advertising medium.

Such campaigns are referred to by staff copywriters and designers as "success stories," and the results of the Paramount ad were so spectacular that the promotion department decided to handle the *King Kong* success story in an unprecedented way. "We usually design a folder or brochure showing how readers respond to an ad and send it to advertisers and potential advertisers in the same field," explains promotion art director Andrew Kner, "but in this case I thought it would be more unusual and appropriate to mail a poster." This decision, which in retrospect seems an admirably original approach to the problem, involved Kner

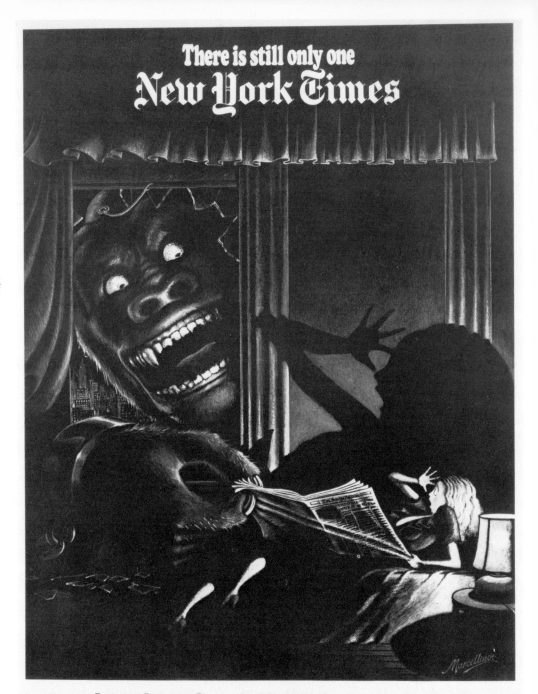

To see how Paramount Pictures found this out in a big way, turn this poster over.

There still is only one King Kong

One year from today Paramount Pictures and Dino De Laurentiis will bring to you the most exciting original motion picture event of all time

King Kong

There still is only one King Kong

One year from today Paramount Pictures and Dino De Laurentiis will bring to you the most exciting original motion picture event of all time

King Kong

When more than 25,000 Times readers wrote for a color reprint of this page advertisement...

Paramount Pictures was "surprised and delighted."

To announce the making of its new motion picture, "King Kong," Paramount Pictures ran a full-page advertisement in the Arts & Leisure section of the Sunday New York Times. A color reprint of the advertisement was offered in small type at the bottom of the page. Steve Rose, Paramount's advertising director, tells what happened.

"Although the opening of King Kong was a year away, we wanted to start stimulating the kind of enthusiasm we felt for the picture. We knew New York Times readers were exceptionally alert and responsive—that's why we chose The Times for our first announcement. But we never expected the response we got.

"We originally assigned one person to handle the requests. On the first day after the ad ran In The Times, we received 200 letters. No problem. But on the second day,

4,000 came in. We had to call in outside help. "The letters came from all over the country, proving again that the Sunday New York Times is a national publication.

"The quality of response was as high as well. We had requests from doctors, lawyers, teachers and all sorts of other professionals. Many people took the time to add personal comments. (One woman wrote, 'Thank you for running a picture of my husband.')

"While the ad was directed to moviegoers, it also gave us exposure to the trade because anybody in the entertainment business has to read The Times, especially the Arts & Leisure section of the Sunday Times.

"When you consider that more than 25,000 people first had to see the ad and spot the

offer in small type, then sit down and write a letter, the response from Times readers was truly remarkable. We're surprised and delighted."

What kind of results can The Times produce for you? You'd be surprised—and delighted. For facts and figures on The Times responsive readership, call Stuart Falk, national advertising manager, at (212) 556-1201 or Lane Beckham, amusement advertising manager, at (212) 556-1847. Or write them at

The New York Times
229 West 43d Street, New York, N.Y. 10036

Other advertising offices of The New York Times

---

in special negotiations both to stretch the budget and wrest approval from recalcitrant superiors who thought the scheme unorthodox.

Basing the Times' headline on Paramount's ad, copywriter Neil Leonard, Kner, and artist Fred Marcellino decided to illustrate the poster with a scene recalling one of the movie's most gripping episodes. "We originally discussed doing a take-off on the Paramount painting depicting King Kong on top of the World Trade Center holding a copy of the Times instead of an airplane," recalls Kner, "but Fred remembered this scene and it

seemed more original." Marcellino, whose humorous style, though contemporary, is enormously effective in appealing to his audience's nostalgia for the '30s, merely substituted the New York Times for Fay Wray as the object of King Kong's pursuit. The story about Paramount's newspaper ad appeared on the poster's reverse side. Kner's first problem was to get approval for four-color printing rarely used in "success story" brochures. That bridge crossed, he set about selling the design to the promotion hierarchy, a group which isn't always open-minded about expensive new approaches to old problems.

"We need as many as eight signatures for design approval," Kner reports, "and there was some fear that this illustration was too strong or too camp for the Times, but we won out."

With luck, the success of this project may make future ventures into unexplored territory easier to manage. "This is an excellent example of the power of a poster," Kner observes. "We have done some lovely brochures as success stories in the past but no one has ever requested copies. These posters were not for sale but they have become such a hot underground item that we have completely run out."

Above, left: original Paramount newspaper ad. Above, right: back of New York Times poster.

Client: The New York Times
Design firm: Promotion Art Department, New York Times, New York
Art director/designer: Andrew Kner
Illustrator/designer: Fred Marcellino
Copywriter: Neil Leonard
Color: Full color
Size: 17″ by 25″

DISCOVER WOLF TRAP!

Wolf Trap Farm Park is a national park and summertime performing arts center in Vienna, Virginia. Because the center is run on a non-profit basis, the directors decided to launch a large-scale fund-raising/advertising campaign to promote its exciting program of cultural events. An important element in the campaign, which was planned around the headline ''Discover Wolf Trap!,'' was a poster to be produced for display in gift shops, record stores and on public bulletin boards where it would attract the attention of potential concert-goers and dance enthusiasts. To insure its success, art director Christine Stansbury-Mueller enlisted the services of Milton Glaser, a designer whose name and reputation she felt to be on a par with those of the world-renowned artists who appear at Wolf Trap each summer.

Glaser was enthusiastic about the assignment. Having recently completed a number of single-image posters, he welcomed the chance provided by the diversity of the Wolf Trap performances to do something more complex. His solution is something of a performance in itself. A multiple-level design which embraces a decorative assortment of miniature *tableaux*, his illustration conjures up sunsets, leafy green shade, people relaxing on a lawn, starry evening skies and the more elusive quality of the ambiance created by the entertainment. The theme is carried out in a rhythmic border motif of trees and moons.

Stansbury-Mueller accepted Glaser's original black-and-white sketch and the client's director of advertising and public relations approved the finished art. The poster's dimensions conform to press sheet size and the final printing was done by offset in an edition of 3000. The only time-consuming element was on-press proofing in two different process reds to maintain the color balance of the original illustration.

The poster was left undated to allow for sales which continued long after the close of the 1975 season. As a final indication of the design's popularity, Glaser's art was converted for use on a T-shirt which has completely sold out.

Client: Wolf Trap Farm Park for the Performing Arts
Design firm: Stansbury: Design, Inc., Greenbelt, MD
Agency: Bill Rolle and Associates, Inc.
Art director/copywriter: Christine Stansbury-Mueller
Designer/illustrator: Milton Glaser
Printer: Garamond-Pridemark Press, Inc.
Colors: Full color
Size: 16" by 24"

Visual History of the Piscataqua

For the opening of its show of photographs culled from the John P. Adams collection, the University of New Hampshire's Art Galleries asked the Office of Publications to produce a poster announcement. Since the poster would function both as an invitation to the exhibit of historical photographs and as general promotion of the University Art Galleries, Ken Silvia's assignment became dual-leveled. The design had to solidly reflect the galleries' image while drawing a wide audience from throughout the state.

In addition to the project's criteria, Silvia was faced with the problem of designing a poster that would be eye-catching in a visually polluted space—in this instance the student bulletin boards of the University—while not exceeding bulletin board size.

Silvia's approach was simple yet compelling. The type is understated, playing up the humor and charm of the visual. "The photo selected had less historical significance than many of the others in the collection but was deliberately chosen because I felt it would appeal to a wide cross section of people," says Silvia. Indeed the poster is a balance of present sophistication and past naiveté and projects a quality feeling to the viewer.

Although there was no time for the luxury of alternate designs, the tricky part took place during the production phase. As the budget ($600) couldn't handle four-color, the poster was done in orange and black duotone surrounded by black solid. "The client insisted that the printed photo color be as close as possible to the sepia used in the glass plate printing process," Silvia points out. "This was difficult to predict with only two colors." Working in offset, he and the printer (whom Silvia terms a "craftsman") ran a second black over the first.—*VFB*

A Visual History
of the
Piscataqua Region:
Early Photographs from
the Personal Collection
of John P. Adams

February 24-March 18, 1976
University Art Galleries
Paul Creative Arts Center
UNH, Durham

Client: University Art Galleries, Paul Arts Center, University of New Hampshire
Design firm: Office of Publications, University of New Hampshire, Durham, NH
Art director/designer: Ken Silvia
Photographer: John P. Adams
Printer: Vermont Graphics
Colors: Black and orange duotone surrounded by black solid
Size: 20" by 30"

The basic physical properties of a poster hardly ever change. The size may vary, of course, and if the budget permits, the printing can be done in 12 colors instead of one or two. But a poster is essentially a large sheet produced specifically to be put up on a wall. That Peter Bradford's poster design for the American Institute of Architect's national convention in Philadelphia in May 1976 capitalized on a new concept in format gives it a special place in the development of promotional graphics. The poster can be hung up in the conventional manner, but an overall network of perforations dividing the sheet into 25 5" by 7" cards carries the announcement into a kind of fourth dimension. ''I don't think it was used whole as much as it was used piecemeal for postcards and stationery,'' Bradford remarks. The story, however, doesn't begin with the perforations.

When AIA convention chairman Richard Saul Wurman asked Bradford to design the announcement, the convention was a full six months away and plans for some of the scheduled activities were still rather hazy. Nevertheless, architects in AIA chapter cities throughout the country had to be notified of the event and encouraged to attend. Wurman gave Bradford all the information about the program that was available and described the ambiance he hoped to create. The theme was to be ''An

1.

1. Final poster.
2. Early idea emphasizing theme of "welcome" to the convention; rejected as too limited, not suggestive of variety of events to be presented.
3. First sketch incorporating symbology of convention events and postcard format; rejected as too pictorial. Bradford feels this probably would have been the best approach had it been possible to use four or five colors.
4. Second postcard sketch; rejected as too corny and simplistic.
5. Sketch done during meeting with client during which Bradford used the words "mosaic, fabric, ball of string" to help client understand his intention to visualize the texture of the convention.

Client: American Institute of Architects
Art director: Peter Bradford
Designers/copywriters: Peter Bradford, Richard Saul Wurman
Printer: Albert H. Vela
Colors: Red and blue on Weyerhaeuser Birch Bark
Size: 24″ by 36″

American City'' and he wanted the graphics to realize visually the variety, the opportunity, the richness—the fabric—of convention week.

Wurman, whose collaboration Bradford welcomed, originally suggested a design incorporating multiple views of different convention activities. Carrying this suggestion one step further, he introduced the idea of postcards which he intended to use as a direct mail campaign inundating potential convention-goers with new information every month. Bradford's first sketches involved pictorial interpretations of the convention activities but were rejected as too literal and simplistic. His final solution, a woven pattern of words printed in red and blue on a beige background, avoided the use of illustrative symbols, which Bradford found disruptive. ''As always, we tried a number of possible solutions before we were sure this final solution offered the most potential,'' Bradford recalls. ''Some of the others tended to reject themselves because they were too difficult to execute properly. Intuitively I felt this one was right,'' he continues; ''when I sketched it during a meeting with the client, it immediately replaced the other ideas. I think more than anything it was the visual aspect of the weave of content that sold it. I used the words 'mosaic, fabric, ball of string' to help the client understand my intent.'' Although the poster was no longer divided into a

pattern of rectangles representing different events, Bradford and Wurman decided to hold onto the postcard idea and simply superimpose the perforated grid over the wavy lines of type.

Bradford's budget was fairly generous—$2000 for all preparatory expenses including type, and $2500 to print 2500 posters. Although the poster was designed ''schematically'' only two days before the mechanical due date, after about two weeks of what Bradford refers to as ''mental distilling,'' he doesn't think that time is an important element in design problems of this sort. ''One always tends to produce the effort right up against the deadline regardless of its proximity,'' he observes.

The poster seems to have been well worth the production problems caused by perforating the paper and printing the reverse side with a postcard format. It was the most successful AIA convention poster to date, its run quickly exhausted by enthusiastic recipients who enjoyed using the mailing cards for promotional, personal and business correspondence and requested additional copies.

In spite of its success, however, Bradford is not entirely satisfied with his design. ''Although it has a pleasant texture,'' he explains candidly, ''I think the design is a little dull and doesn't entice you to read the rather complex typography. Small pictorial elements could have helped.''

Sam Davis/Robert Mangurian

As a rule, there is very short notice when guests are lined up to appear at the UCLA School of Architecture and Urban Planning. For that reason, program announcements must be prepared with unusual speed.

Coy Howard's poster for the Sam Davis/Robert Mangurian lectures was no exception: Howard was notified of the earlier Sam Davis lecture ten days prior to the event. This left him with one day for design and production and three days for printing. The balance of time was needed for mailing the poster to members of the professional architecture and design communities in Southern California. (The poster was also to be placed on the UCLA campus where it would be seen by a good percentage of the university's 30,000 students.) The budget was hardly on a grand scale, either. Howard was allotted $150 to work with.

The time/money situation facing Howard meant utilizing "on-hand" or "found" images, as well as those that were quickly produced. He also had to cope with the fact that he had been given only the titles of the lectures and knew virtually nothing about the actual topics Davis and Mangurian would discuss. Beyond these problems, though, Howard wanted to step outside the architecture-bound graphic range, something he has attempted in his previous posters for the School of Architecture. As he expresses it, "I look for imagery that can both exist on its own and serve to

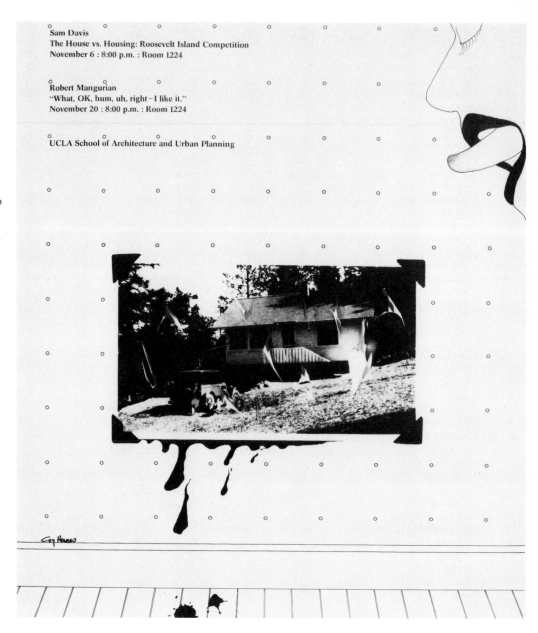

Sam Davis
The House vs. Housing: Roosevelt Island Competition
November 6 : 8:00 p.m. : Room 1224

Robert Mangurian
"What, OK, hum, uh, right – I like it."
November 20 : 8:00 p.m. : Room 1224

UCLA School of Architecture and Urban Planning

Opposite page: original sketches made on a yellow legal pad with green felt-tipped pen.

suggest and support multiple interpretations of the lecture topics." Indeed, since graphic designers also receive the school's posters, the use of broader visual concepts becomes important.

From his extremely rough sketches which experimented with the open mouth, protruding tongue and photograph in various positions, Howard derived his final design combining the "found" photograph with pen and ink. As he puts it, the composition "seemed to 'push' the lecture topics into a provocative and enigmatic dialogue." Curiously, since the school provided only the most essential information, there is no way of telling from the poster if the connection between the two lectures is real or invented by the design.

Printed in sepia on white translucent parchment and hand-tinted in pink, yellow and blue-green colored pencil, the yawning face seems to be a visual interpretation of Mangurian's title, "What, OK, hum, uh, right—I like it." The photograph obviously relates to "The House vs. Housing." Only their arrangement against a background suggesting the wall of a room relates the images, although the knife slashes, sensually protruding tongue, and drops of blood unite to make the poster visually provocative in spite of the prosaic titles of the lectures. Howard stresses that the poster's function was to bring forth the concept that an event was taking place within the School of

Architecture. What he calls "more discreet forms of announcements" have been tried but do not draw as large an audience of professionals and students. Aside from drawing attention to the announcement, Howard's hand-made slashes serve to comment on the painful nature of memories associated with certain architectural settings, and also symbolize the vandalism of an already deteriorating house.

Howard notes that the poster marked a "design breakthrough" for him. The imagery is quite sparse in comparison with his previous work, and it was the first time the concept had included the manipulation of the piece after printing.—*VFB*

Client: University of California at Los Angeles, School of Architecture and Urban Planning
Art director/designer/ illustrator: Coy Howard, Los Angeles
Printer: Continental Graphics
Colors: Sepia with hand-colored pink, yellow, blue-green
Size: 18¾" by 22¼"

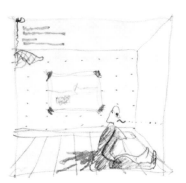

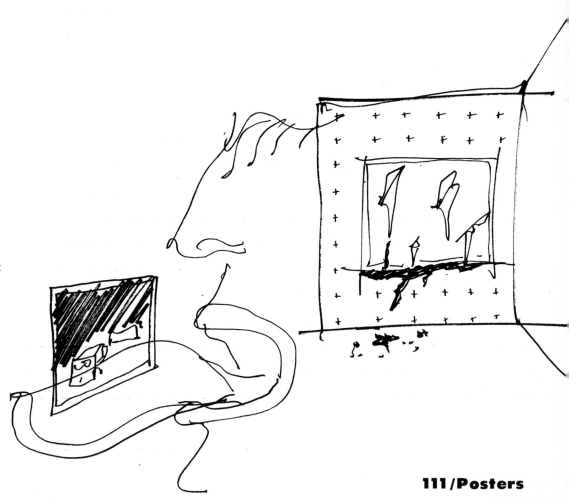

Cities Are Neighborhoods

A national conference on neighborhood conservation was held in New York City during the fall of 1975. Sponsored by an impressive collection of government agencies including the National Endowment for the Arts and the Landmarks Preservation Commission of the City of New York, the conference consisted of workshops, symposiums and lectures which would highlight the need for sensitive and concerted action to conserve the older neighborhoods of America's urban centers.

To invite some 350 distinguished participants and give them information about the program, the conference sponsors required a comprehensive inventory of printed material. Prepared by Stephen Geissbuhler of Chermayeff & Geismar Associates, these items consisted of a preliminary announcement, the listing of events, the conference letterhead, a button, and a book. For the cover of the program, he chose a photograph depicting row upon row of two-story frame houses advancing in a steady rhythmic progression upon the massive, towering skyscrapers of a central city. "We sifted through a lot of stock photos for the conference book," Geiss-buhler recalls. "This seemed the best image for the topic we were talking about and it was compatible with the typographic design of the other pieces."

After the conference was over, its sponsors felt strongly that the people who had been present ought to be reminded in as durable a manner as possible that the issue of neighborhood conservation and revitalizing the cities should not be forgotten even though the symposiums and workshops had come to an end. As a follow-up effort, the National Endowment for the Arts asked Chermayeff & Geismar to create a poster which could be mailed to city, state, and federal officials, architects and planners, economists and sociologists, lawyers, developers, and

bankers who had attended. Basing his design on the same photograph he had used for the program and book covers, Geissbuhler put together, in one day, an image unrecognizable as any specific city, which symbolized both the positive and negative aspects of the contemporary urban landscape. Using black ink, Geissbuhler extensively worked over and simplified a kodalith made from the original halftone print. He then superimposed a positive film of the resulting black-and-white line art on a positive print of the same line image and shifted it slightly out of register. The final printing was done in two blacks—one matte and one glossy. According to Geissbuhler, many people

Program cover.

have requested posters for framing and permanent display, a fair indication that the issue of neighborhood conservation is neither out of sight nor out of mind.

Client: National Endowment for the Arts
Design firm: Chermayeff & Geismar Associates, New York
Art directors: Ivan Chermayeff, Stephan Geissbuhler
Designer: Stephan Geissbuhler
Photographer: Elliot Erwitt/Magnum
Printer: Crafton Graphic Co.
Colors: Dull and glossy black
Size: 22" by 26¾"